BEAUTY
for
ASHES

THE VIRTUOUS SIDE OF FAILURE

DR. PIERRE McDONNAUGH

Fulton Books
Meadville, PA

Published by Fulton Books 2022

ISBN 979-8-88505-185-9 (paperback)
ISBN 979-8-88731-544-7 (hardcover)
ISBN 979-8-88505-186-6 (digital)

Printed in the United States of America

To the great many individuals that were instrumental in helping me along the way like Peter Camejo; Brian Moss; John Delehaye; David Vaughn; Ricky Marciano; Toby Hecht; DeÁna H. Dow; Sandra Nicotra; Jim Johnston; Michelle Cenis, who promoted me at every turn and convinced me that I was a rock star; and Daron, Dylan, Stiles, and Chase for being the best children ever.

CONTENTS

ILLUSTRATIONS

INTRODUCTION

If I ran the whole place like it was my way or the highway, we would not be as good a company. I'm going to have mistakes — they'll be made on my watch and embarrass me. But I'll also make sure the company learns from them so it can be a better company.

—Jamie Dimon,

The key to unlocking the powers behind the virtues of failure is to first, above all things, be kind to ourselves. Anyone with a dream will be visited upon by failure in their lifetime because it is an integral part of the process. Whether it be in your ambitions, which, by the way, are completely controlled by us, or in life generally, where mistakes seemingly happen spontaneously. It's necessary that we habitually forgive ourselves for our mistakes while we persistently strive to get it right. For in the end, the cumulative shame of our failures may rob us of our joy and take us backward. A shame that lends to an irrational, unsustainably high definition of what it means to be competent. Love yourself, be kind to yourself, and always forgive yourself.

1

THE TRUE NATURE OF FAILURE

To bestow on them a crown of beauty instead of ashes,

the oil of joy instead of mourning, and a garment

of praise instead of a spirit of despair.

—Isaiah 61:3

ou are a failure of the grandest proportions…or at least you should be! Failure is in all of us. It's how we learn. Failure is the silence between the notes; it's the darkness against which the foreground exists and is thereby a significant and the most necessary feature of our collective ambition. The actual fact is that we are all failures as we have failed many times in our lives. However, we have not categorized our experiences with failure as such, and it has remained concealed from

our conscious awareness. We grew up learning through trial and error and became self-conscious, arrogant, proud, and fragile. We became shocked at our infallibility, and it was at that time we clung tightly to our cumulative achievements, fearful of losing ground, and stopped learning from our shortcomings...and our ambition began to die. How did we reach such a sad state of affairs? It's like holding a fistful of sand; no matter how tightly we cling and squeeze, it just pours out between our fingers, leaving our hands empty in the end. We must face the uncertainty and fear of loss in order to break free and keep moving toward our best selves. Only then can we find the edge, test the boundaries again, and muster the courage to start failing again if we are to continue growing and becoming what we are meant to be in this life.

Personally, I have always felt like a "successful failure." Although this may sound like an oxymoron, I should explain; looking back, I have had many experiences—good and bad. I have travelled along many paths and made decisions that led me in many different directions, not all of which entirely according to plan. Notwithstanding all the trials and tribulations, I am quite satisfied with where I now find myself: a corporate attorney working at a major investment bank, a licensed financial services professional, professor of wealth management, a former college athlete, a US Air Force veteran, and a father of four amazing boys. However, regardless of what actually happened in my life, who I have become is determined solely by how I characterize myself through my experiences. How we characterize our life experiences is projected onto how others see us via our self-image. For example, if we are very good in math but horrible in writing, what do we tell people about who we are? Is it "Hi, I am Pierre, and I am a horrible writer" or "Hi, I am Pierre, and I am excellent in math"?

I always used to highlight to anyone that would listen that I was terrible in math (even though I sold investments to high-net-worth investors for a living), though I would never mention that I was an excellent architectural draftsman, writer, athlete, or artist or any other good thing about myself. Putting myself in the best light in this manner is a lesson that came to me far too late in life, as I regularly described myself by my shortcomings and failings as if that's who I was. All too often, I characterized myself as a failure as I failed to graduate from junior high school and high school, resulting in my inability to play NCAA basketball because I was always academically ineligible. It took me well over four years to complete my undergraduate degree, and I barely got into law school after I changed careers (largely due to a failed marriage that ended in the suicide of my spouse). This book is about failure and how I came to contextualize the importance of failure in pursuing my ambition. It also takes a deeper look at the many virtues of failure, or the lessons that we only learn in hindsight, when we make the effort and fall short of success. These are invaluable lessons that can only be understood in the context of failure. I say this is my story because I learned all too late that there was any value in my experiences with failure and, as a result, missed out on the wisdom of the experiences until much later in life. They say hindsight is twenty-twenty; however, to learn from it requires that you look back, which most of us don't do because of the shame associated with failing.

For me, it would be growing up alongside a brother only one year older than me but light years ahead in terms of his intellectual development that contributed greatly to my feelings of inadequacy. Whether it was football, basketball, ping-pong in our dad's basement, or the chess club at school, I lost to him again and again. He was at the top of his music class with the trumpet while I got kicked out of violin for not keeping up. He was a sports legend while I could barely make teams. Teachers would regularly come to me, praising his name often—the same teachers that removed me from class for being disruptive. We could not be more different. Culture played a major role in this phenomenon as well, as there is a preference toward the older siblings in terms of latitude and support for their activities in families such as mine. With me being the youngest child, I didn't stand a chance at recognition within the pecking order. Characterizing myself as a failure came easy in such a cultural setting as it reinforced the treatment that was already being meted out. It provided a ready-to-hand explanation as to why I was being disregarded. Even when I achieved something worthy of note, it would gain no traction among the preexisting order within my family. For example, at twelve years old, I was enrolled in tech shop at school, the objective of which was toward developing architectural understanding and drafting skills while designing from scratch and building a small-scale model home. This was a very intricate undertaking as it involved cutting and measuring the studs, joints, headers, etc. to scale size and constructing the entire project from the foundation on up. The entire project took the full school year, and my model was a contender for an award as the most creative. It was based on a modified A-frame ski-chalet-style structure. I was so proud as it came together; I thought I could not wait until my parents saw not only the finished product but that it would win the top design concept for the class.

The course came to an end, and the house was complete. It was so big, I brought it home with the help of a friend. Although I was an *A* student in tech shop, the project was met with lukewarm enthusiasm by my family. I kept it on display in my room for a while, but my mother allowed my younger brother to play with it as a dollhouse. Infuriated, I thought this would not do, so I asked my dad to keep it as his house. Unbeknownst to me, he kept it in his basement along with a random assortment of junk, and it ultimately was destroyed and thrown out.

Apparently, my best was still not good enough. Culturally, this was a setting where the only way you could be recognized was not by objectively doing well but by satisfying the role that was set for you within the system. For me, that was the role of the loser, or as John Bradshaw calls the scapegoat (John Bradshaw, *Healing the Shame That Binds You*, part one, PBS). Scapegoats are children blamed for all the problems in dysfunctional families. The term comes from the book of Leviticus in the Bible, where the Israelites conduct a ceremony in which they direct their sins onto an escape goat and subsequently set it free into the wilderness to cleanse the wickedness from their community. The scapegoat bears the burden of taking on the misdeed of a tribe, community, or family. The reasons for this are myriad (e.g., a parent might prefer the child who brings the most glory to the family while scapegoating the child who does not boosts the family's public image). It can be equally as tough to know the exact reasons for it, as it is difficult for a child to shrug off this role and get the attention it needs to thrive as a kid, if not impossible. The tendency is for most similarly situated children in such circumstances to result in an upbringing where the scapegoated child's inherent worth, goodness, and lovableness are ignored, leading him to just accept the role and run with it. In my case, I became a self-professed class clown and was quite funny too! I regularly got kicked out of class, received after-school detentions, and got lots of *F*s.

I enjoyed my lot in life as it got me the attention I sought but only up until a certain point—short of being respected and mattering. Achieving my dreams meant not only escaping that system but more importantly becoming dead to my old self and starting all over again among strangers. The Bible refers to this as "putting off the old man," which belongs to your former manner of life (Ephesians 4:22 ESV). In this way, I would come to understand that failure was not what I thought it was and that there was a great deal of value in failing. By taking responsibility for who I have become, I could uncouple my concept of failure from the shame that dominated my experience with it. As John Bradshaw observed, "the most paradoxical aspect of neurotic shame is that it is the core motivator of the super-achieved and the underachieved, the star and the scapegoat, the righteous and the wretched, the powerful and the pathetic." This brought about in me a shame-based false identity as a failure, and it was constraining me from becoming my whole self, my divine self—the self I was indented to be. Starting out life as a shame-based failure was a heavy burden for any young person to bear, as this identity would become crystalized within me, causing an unconscious move from a healthy shame to a toxic shame-based identity. Years of therapy would reveal that this transition brought with it a shift in the core of my being so painful to bear (consciously) that I developed a false sense of self. This is the tragedy that occurs to many young people, precluding them from being the whole people we were meant to be. This is how we go from being perfect children to losing the childlike mood of wonder as adults. It comes on gradually and unconsciously through this process of emotional battering or neglect; and ultimately, we concede to depression, complacency, and beyond. In time, the core belief about ourselves becomes "We are flawed failures."

According to Bradshaw, all disorders start out this way—rooted in toxic shame. The one sorrow in life is that we fall short of our own expectations when we don't become the people we were meant to be. In fact, the crisis of most families is the universal human problem of maintaining a wrong perception of ourselves, and in one sense, that's the only problem that people have: the lost sense of self. We all seem to have a wrong belief about ourselves, and out of that wrong belief comes "wrong choosing," as the choices we make in life depend on the what we believe. For example, our belief about the world will inform how we will react to the world we end up creating. The world that we believe is out there, and if we believe it is no good, it will be no good, as we create that world by possessing a correlating attitude even when there is data to the contrary. Studies have shown that we discount our experiences to make them fit our belief systems. In essence, whatever we believe about ourselves is going to be the map that we use to make every other decision about our life.

Yes, for want of understanding this, things were difficult for me from the start, and as a kid, I had no idea of the impact this would have on my journey. However, as seductive a solution it would be to just sit back and blame the world for my early shortcomings, it would not be entirely accurate. For, what accounted most for my experiences was more an issue of the stories I told myself about me, or at least the story that I settled upon—the narrative about who I was to me. What I failed to realize back then was that the goal of any narrative was for me to feel better about myself and that anything I did to make myself feel better was perfectly acceptable. I could not function effectively, much less joyously, unless I regained a sense of success and self-esteem, and that reinterpretation of my own past to put it in the most positive light was simply good for my mental health.

The fact of the matter was that there was no objective truth in what happened to me (or any of us, for that matter) as all stories are told by a narrator, and in this case, I was both narrator and audience. If as a narrator, you constantly tell yourself a negative story, you as the audience feel sad and powerless. However, if as narrator, you downplay the negative events and emphasize the hero's accomplishments, you as the audience are likely to be inspired. The events have not changed, only the narration. The main reason it is important to reinterpret your past in this way, in the most positive empowering way, is that it enables you to rewrite your story the way it was intended and in the way that works. At first, reinventing a new narrative may sound very strange; however, you must ask yourself where your story came from in the first place. Concluding that it came from somewhere else (e.g., family, history, religion, etc.) seems to make it closer to truth for some reason.

The starting point of my personal transformation was that I had to change the narrative about myself that was continuously running in the background of my mind and run a new, revised script. As long as I was stuck in a negative interpretation of myself, I had invested a great deal of time in anxiously worrying and yielding my power to wishing and hoping. Fernando Flores once said that, "hope is the raw material of losers", and we all know that worrying can become a full- time occupation. Negative interpretations and ruminations that lead to worrying can cripple you. Positive interpretations give you energy to go on with your life. In other words, reinterpreting your story is practical.

When I recast the narrative in my favor, it became clear to me that, while I may have been failing, the real value was in my efforts, in that I was trying. I was making the effort and persevering. What mattered, contrary to popular belief, was not how I started but how I finished. We tend to put an inordinate amount of energy behind who got into which university, who was at the top of the class, who got into which company and program, etc., but we seldom hear about the backward-looking glance of who persevered and where people subsequently ended up. What happened to the valedictorian after graduation, the star athlete once he left the game, the CEO or president when they left the company, etc.? For each step along the way, there were two sides of my story, as is the case with most of us. We struggle, and if we persevere, we overcome. And then we craft the narrative through the lens of our self-image, which can be either negative or positive. The bottom line, however, is that succeeding is a process, and what happens along the way—key word: *happens*—be it good or bad, either works or doesn't work. Through it all, failure and correction are an integral part of that process. Whether, in our lives, we are the hero or the scapegoat, it all comes down to our perspective, our attitude toward ourselves, and our self-image. Our perspective, however, is largely influenced by our family, culture, traditions, and early life choices—the consequences of which we tend to be stuck with. At that point, when I took control of the story of my life, I began to reorder how I understood the success and failure of me. I wrote a new script not full of positive, forward-looking aspirations but of truths and valuable characteristics that my community never recognized in me and that I never saw in myself. These were characteristics that were always present within me but never highlighted, supported, or encouraged. I began to encourage myself and focus on what I did right, no longer reinforcing what I did wrong. I began to allow myself to try and fail without judgment to learn from those failures instead of living through the embarrassment and shame of it. I learned to forgive myself for falling short, with the understanding that we are constantly becoming something new as human beings. And there was a degree of mystery in that, but we should trust the process nonetheless. This would require a great deal of courage and humility on my part in order for me to continue to become what I would become and learn lessons from my experiences and my failures.

Success, as we are all familiar with, is a way of living founded on benefiting from all life has to offer. It is a long-term sequence of life-improving results and a process of continual development, learning, and fulfillment in living. Success is also an opportunity for learning and development, creative change, and innovation, which may include an outcome of short-term setbacks and failures. However it is defined, any true definition of what success is must incorporate failure as an integral part of the process. True success can only be built on a solid sense of self. It comes from striking a balance between who you are and what we do, establishing the innocence of value so that only ourselves and not others may judge our work and our worth.

We have to learn to take joy in the process of what we do rather than its outcome. True success then may involve a fundamental reappraisal of self, a reshuffling of the pieces, and a painful look inside. But what makes us undertake such a difficult endeavor? Generally, only through a setback such as failure are we moved to reexamine ourselves in such a deep and meaningful way. The real successes among us, in other words, are often people who have learned from the lessons of failure. This is the true power of failure.

The power of failure

Make no mistake. This book is a story about failure, the "virtues of failure," in fact, and this is my story. Failure, for too long, has largely been a misunderstood concept. Although its significance has been accepted by a somewhat narrow contingent of people worldwide, understanding its value has yet to take root in the public discourse. Athletes, soldiers, salesmen, entrepreneurs, and children will understand these principles quite well. Everyone else, not so much. What these people understand about failure is that its occurrence in our lives is inevitable when moving toward our ultimate objective. Whether it's becoming proficient at "getting vertical" on a half-pipe with a skateboard, making top sales revenue for the quarter, being voted MVP during the playoff game, or pushing your body to its absolute limit during Operation Red Flag, not only is it necessary to fail; it's the only way to find your outer bounds—going to that place you never were before to find your personal limit and pushing it to a whole new level. This is where superstars are made and entrepreneurs turn good unique ideas into billions; it's where children have the time of their lives and writers make history.

Unfortunately, this is also where we experience crushing bouts of disappointment in ourselves and shame in the face of our friends, family, and communities. Although failure is important, it's even more important that we experience failure in its proper perspective: in that "When I fail" does not mean "I am a failure." We must not allow our situation to define our identity. As much as this may appear to be a common-sense understanding, we still have to reconcile this understanding within our individual cultural settings as well as we are all part of social systems of rules that we did not create nor control. This is to say that no matter how new-age we are in our thinking, we still belong to and thrive in networks of others that may not understand nor agree with our desire to become better selves. Along with this comes a dire consequence for violating the codes and tra-

15

ditions as we begin to change who we are in fundamental ways. This presents a major impediment to our transcendence. Our notions of failure reside all too often within a cultural context and hence must be understood from that perspective as well. The following is primarily written as a message in a bottle for my children, friends, and colleagues to help them understand that they must have the courage to fail and the patience to recover in order to become their best selves, to never be afraid to expend the effort it takes to be great at their chosen avocation, or to move into an uncertain direction. In the words of the Roman emperor Marcus Aurelius, "Within every obstacle is an opportunity to improve our condition," and that it is, in fact, "the obstacle in the path becomes the path." Presented within these pages is a recharacterization of how failure functions in the context of our ambitions as it must be understood as the foundation of success and the means by which it can be achieved (Lao Tzu).

Culture and traditions

As mentioned above, the degree to which we associate the act of failing with ourselves as failures appear to be reinforced culturally as attitudes to failure are often related to a culture's attitude to risk.

Culture may be construed to represent a phenomenon of immense complexity in that it seeks to articulate the understanding of society. Culture may also be seen to represent social variables that range from knowledge to language and customs, thus defining how humans interact with society. At the core of the articulation of culture are constructs such as ideas, norms, and beliefs of institutions, groups, and primarily, the individual.

Dealing with failure and learning from it is, in many cases, our key to success. Yet understanding failure and the way it is perceived is important when working in a cross-cultural setting. However, different cultures have completely opposing attitudes to failure. For example, in the USA, where risk and entrepreneurship are admired and winners reap big financial rewards, failure is seen as a mere bump in the road to success. Yet in Japan, failing in a business venture can be fatal to a person's professional reputation. The chief executive of a failed enterprise is expected to apologize personally for letting people down. It would be unwise to share stories of your business failures with Japanese colleagues in the hope of bonding over shared experiences. The most likely outcome would be a loss of face for you and great embarrassment for your colleagues. In Germany, however, where the social fabric is held together by a series of rules and laws and long-term security is prized, failure is seen as weak and ineffi-cient. According to a report by ARN (*Australian IT News* channel), even Australians are regarded as conservative both in business and as consumers. It is believed that Islamic cultures, very broadly speaking, are likely to be less tolerant of failure. In a world where personal con-tacts and relationships take precedence over business with strangers, where maintaining harmony and face are crucial, and where strict hierarchy, risk aversion, and fatalism are commonplace, there is lit-tle room for experimentation and failure. The more conservative the culture the less tolerance for failure. Saudi Arabia, for example, is not known for its entrepreneurial spirit.

Although, in a surprising twist, the multicultural United Arab Emirates is a society increasingly open to encouraging entrepreneurs, which might suggest that attitudes toward failure are mellowing. India, too, is fast emerging as a country of opportunists and entre-preneurs. India's education system does not necessarily foster the lateral thinking, imagination, and self-motivation required to be an entrepreneur; and failure, historically, is seen as a disaster, even affect-ing an individual's family name and marriage prospects. But accord-ing to *Reuters*, India's technology boom, fueled by the availability of venture-capital cash and a Silicon Valley mentality, is dramatically changing attitudes toward failure. Be it culture, religion, or tradition, attitudes toward failure must be taken into consideration in producing a shift or recharacterization toward how failure is viewed on an individual level. However insurmountable it may seem, culture is more of an obstacle than an impediment to shifting attitudes toward failure and risk, as evidenced by events in Mexico. Ironically, it was in a Latin culture, where there is little tolerance for failure and the loss of face it brings, that a global movement was launched in 2012. In Mexico, where 75 percent of start-ups close after two years, a group of friends, all of whom had experienced failure in business at some point, founded FUN—a series of events that has now spread to one hundred cities worldwide, at which business people stand up and talk frankly about their failures, which is followed by a Q and A. Worldwide, ten thousand people attend these events every month.

Closely behind culture, impacting our commonly held perceptions of failure, is tradition. It is widely understood that every question grows out of a tradition—a preunderstanding that opens the space of possible answers. We use the word *tradition* here in a broad sense without the connotation that it belongs to a cohesive social or cultural group or that it consists of particular customs or practices. Tradition is a more pervasive, fundamental phenomenon that might be called a way of being. In trying to understand a tradition, the first thing we have to become aware of is how it is concealed by its obviousness. It is not a set of rules or sayings or something we will find catalogued in an encyclopedia. Traditions are a way of under-standing—a background within which we interpret and act. We use the word *tradition* because it emphasizes the historicity of our ways of thinking—the fact that we always exist within a preunderstanding determined by the history of our interactions with others who share the tradition. When we encounter people who live in a substantially different tradition all the time, we are struck by the impression that they have a strange and apparently arbitrary worldview. It takes a careful self-awareness to turn the same gaze on our own lives and unconceal our own traditions to bring into conscious observation that which invisibly gives shape to our own thoughts.

In fact, traditions, along with culture and religion, can be a hidden source of failure in that we accept them wholesale and unex-amined. The classic Freudian view of truth regards tradition nega-tively as that which, on the basis of unwarranted authority, blinds us to a realistic perception of the world. What defines a tradition is that those who espouse it or abide by it accept certain ideas or practices unreflectively, or at least reflection is not what determines their acceptance. What is decisive is rather that these ideas and practices have in some sense been handed down by previous generations. Traditions are thrust upon us from past generations usually through a form of group enculturation, lending the ideas and practices their authority. But at the same time, we know that traditions brought forward in this way do not actually make ideas true or practices justified or prove them to be so in anyway. It may make us take traditional ideas and practices for granted (the past and our upbringing indeed have a strong hold). But the fact of the matter is that the ideas of the generations of our fathers are no truer by virtue of their being ideas of earlier generations. Here, the tension between truth and tradition comes to the fore. While tradition is a major source of unquestioned preconceptions, for truth to be attained, these preconceptions rooted in traditions must be overcome. It is in this way the tradition conceals truth objectively and subjectively and precludes our ability to see our experiences clearly and to learn from them when that experience is failure.

Failure defined

Although there appears to be no objectively verifiable definition of *failure*, each experience with it appears to be unique to each of us. Our response to it, however, is often the same: fear, frustration, confusion, despair, shame, and even nihilism and anger. Carole Hyatt and Linda Gottlieb, in their book *When Smart People Fail* (1987), define failure as a judgement of events, although it is commonly understood differently. Emphasizing the relationship of failure to events, they provided the example of how a job loss is merely an event but can be seen as a great relief if you hated the job; in itself, it is only an event, not a failure. It only becomes a failure if you or someone else viewing it decides it is a failure. The problem here is that the word *failure* has been so closely linked to the events themselves that it has come to mean those very events. Others define failure as a short-term unexpected result that reflects a challenge in progress, and that provides a stepping stone to success: it's an opportunity for learning and development and an opportunity for creative change and innovation. We have been led to believe that failure is an objective experience as opposed to a subjective assessment by the one making the judgement. However you define it, what's clear is that we must recharacterize failure (and success, for that matter) as failure is a natural part of life that can impact us positively or negatively depending on how we conceptualize the experience. The distinction between your judgment of the events and the events themselves is a very important one.

This distinction was made clear in the Netflix special *Naomi Osaka*. She was being interviewed on how she felt after losing the 2019 US Open to Belinda Bencic, effectively dropping her rank to no. 4 in the world. Osaka said, "For so long I tied my winning to my worth as a person, [and] to anyone that would know me, they would know me as a tennis player. So what am I worth if I am not a good tennis player?" I completely understood her sentiment and could not agree with her more. In fact, our performance is not what we are. Rick Warren once said in his book *A Purpose Driven Life: What on Earth Am I Here For?* that we are not human doings but human beings. This is critical to keep in mind in any given undertaking because at the end of the day, we are responding to our own ambition. Ambition lies in our wants and desires. As such, ambition is a self-induced pressure that we control and can get out from under at any given point in time. For this reason, we cannot ever "fail" at this so long as we patiently allow ourselves time to achieve our objectives, which, incidentally, is why perseverance is integral to success—to allow ourselves to learn from failure.

Failure is a temporary state whereby our results don't equate to our expectations in spite of our efforts. It is a perception as opposed to a reality that you fell short in some meaningful way; however, the mental and emotional impact and consequences thereof are very real, albeit put in motion by oneself. Failure is not something to be feared as it contains the seeds of tomorrow's greatest successes. Also, failure is more of a subjective phenomenon with subsequently objective consequences that only become crystalized on the cessation of one's efforts. It can only exist once you quit. Failure is temporal as the negative consequences of which become less likely with the passage of time, provided you continue to persist in your efforts. However, what enables this persistence and what makes us vulnerable to quitting seems to have everything to do with our early life experiences. In any case, I don't agree with the view that failure should be destroyed conceptually under the guise of the "Everyone is a winner" ethos, but it should be recharacterized from how it is currently perceived: as a negative, fatal, and final result indicating an inability to perform and a lack of success; a falling short because of ineptness, deficiency, or negligence; and a bad, bad thing that should be avoided, mourned, and punished.

We all learned as children that rewards came with risks as no mother raises a child to walk without letting them fall. I recall being an avid skater when I was young. As I was a teen growing up in New York in the '70s, there were very few, if any, skate parks. We would regularly sneak into a local park at night to skate in an Olympic-size swimming pool that was then under construction. On one end, it was four feet deep, and the other was as deep as twenty feet—perfect for skating. After we hopped the fence and swept the pool of debris, we were off and skating. Initially, the goal was to get "vertical" and then to catch air (or ride off the twenty-foot lip) and do tricks in midair above the edge of the pool. I was determined to get vertical one night. After two attempts, I did it. I got vertical fifteen feet up the wall, just crossing that point where the curvature of the pool stops, hence the name vertical. I was so excited and wanted to relish in the moment. It was then I froze—sideways on the wall—fifteen feet aboveground. I was facing the stars, and in my joy, I inadvertently kicked the board out from under my feet. I came crashing down on my back! Luckily, I had full gear on (helmet, pads, etc.). The takeaway that night was not to focus on the abject horror of falling backward fifteen feet or even the ensuing pain (once my breathing resumed) but on what not to do next time: to maintain focus. That's the only way through to becoming better and enjoying the sport.

For years, I too, failed many, many times and thought I was the failure, but I was wrong. The good thing is I had the wherewithal to stay engaged and keep trying. I knew that if anybody could win, I could win. Unfortunately, so many of us quit before this realization. Bill Gates said, "Once you embrace unpleasant news not as negative but as evidence of a need for change, you aren't defeated by it. You're learning from it." This is what Dr. Charles Manz calls learning forward through failure.

As for Osaka, largely owing to her perseverance, in 2021, she went on to become one of only three players in the Open Era to win her first four Grand Slam finals alongside Roger Federer and Monica Seles. Failure is a significant part of successful living, and its value is in the learning and growth that it provides. Without learning and growth, failure can be a destructive force in our lives. In growing as individuals, we must enter unfamiliar spaces that not only provide us with new experiences, knowledge, and capabilities but also bring with them new opportunities to fail and learn from that ever-present failure. We must remember that hidden within each and every obstacle lies an opportunity to practice patience, courage, humility, resourcefulness, reason, justice, and creativity. We just need to love ourselves, be kind to ourselves, and seek the lessons embedded within our failures and push past them on the next try. And we will be successful in our endeavors.

The etymology of failure

It's hard to imagine that things were not always this way, but modern conceptualizations of failure actually have an origin like most things, and it's a pretty recent one. As early as the Middle Ages, people did not talk of failure. The ups and downs in life were attributed largely to luck, chance, fortune, the will of God, etc. Failure was directly associated with risk, being able to move from the niche into which you were born in order to try something new. In the rigid class system of Europe, where you were expected to do what your father had done before you, the notion of personal failure was almost unthinkable. In addition, the medieval period placed little emphasis on the individual, unique human, and without the glorification of self, there can be no conception of personal success or failure. The architects of the great cathedrals of the Middle Ages neither sought nor received personal fame. The scribes who painstakingly illuminated the medieval manuscripts remained anonymous. The renaissance bequeathed upon us a concept basic to the idea of success: glory. Dante, Petrarch, and the Renaissance poets were stars of their time and proud of their achievements. Ordinary people, too, sought glory not in the afterlife but now. A merchant class was formed, living by their wits, prizing not land or titles but money. In countless Renaissance portraits, these newly successful businessmen proudly show off the jewels, clothing, and furniture they accumulated. In the individualism of the Renaissance, the growth of commerce (and later the antiorthodoxy of the Protestant Reformation) took place, and the seeds of the success-failure ethic were sown. But Europe's entrenched class system prevented those seeds from taking root.

However, in America, everyone was a newcomer, and there were no classes as such. The promise of America was that no matter where you came from, you could end up very wealthy. With no feudal aristocracy to think of, America invented a new upper class with only one entry requirement: money. And since the accumulation of money was open to all, a pervasive American dream was born: upward mobility. Puritan leaders inveighed against the sins of luxury, but even their own Calvinist theology taught that God had given every man a calling. If a man did his calling so well as to amass wealth from it, was that not a sign of God's favor? Besides, how could Puritan leaders tell their followers to accept poverty when the richest land in the world was just outside their doors? In a uniquely American mix, godliness and commerce became forever intertwined, and the Protestant work ethic was born. The business of America would forevermore be business. Subsequent to which, the self-made man sprang forth as a uniquely American invention whereby you could go out and enjoy life, liberty, and the pursuit of wealth guilt-free. God himself had sanctioned it, and the prize for success was something that could never have been his in Europe: immediate entry into the upper class. It was thus with the Puritans the success-failure ethic was born as well.

Biological roots of failure

What we call failure is often a misrepresentation about the difference between what exists and goes unnoticed (such as growth and learning when we fall short of reaching a goal) and what is realized later (longer-term success). The reality is that challenges are just disguised opportunities, differences are a gift, and mistakes are learning opportunities. And when we try our best and are willing to learn, we always succeed even if we don't achieve the results we hoped for.

Failure does not just emerge in cultural perspectives on goal achievement, but it also resides innately as part of our biological makeup and how we make sense of the world around us. The significance of failure is necessary to the makeup of our human biology and a motivating force behind any successful endeavor. Each one of us is a biologically open system that continuously exchanges stimulus and sensory phenomena through touch, taste, smell, sight, and sound with our environment. We may sense the temperature through skin and make adjustments in comfort accordingly. Each one of us experiences the world through our senses, gathering data as we move through space and time. This data is gathered and converted into information of different types as it is consumed by the individual. It may come by way of oxygen conversion to carbon dioxide, nutrients and minerals in food and water converted to energy, or even sensorimotor information lending to decisions about where to go, when to fight or run, and generally, how to survive a given environment. We move not in a straight line toward our goals and objectives, however, but in an iterative fashion, making many minute corrections along the way based on updated sensory information. These sequential iterative corrections cannot be viewed as failures but directional segments that, when strung together, form the path upon which we must travel to reach any given objective. These segments, of course, are based on the information and data we have available at any given point in time, and as we learn and acquire new knowledge and information, correction can be made in our allotted course. However, our reliance on such information, albeit misguided, is required in the completion of our trajectory. It may delay us in the end or even lead to incorrect outcomes, but as our mind is iterative in nature, through continual gathering of data and information processing, corrections will continue until our goals are met. Those of us that push this process more aggressively will develop faster than those who do not; basically, with practices in direction, we can become more efficient at sniffing out opportunities for our collective survival while fearing or misunderstanding failure may just slow us down.

W. Richard Scott (2007), "Organizations and Organizing: Rational, Natural and Open Systems Perspectives", puts forward that among the common characteristics of open systems is the importation of energy, whereby any system that imports energy from outside itself is an open system. By analogy, each of us has patterns of activity that repeat and can be studied in relation to the "energy in, product out" cycle. This energy can be in the form of calories, light, motivation of workers, raw materials, etc.—everything used in the process of turning things into something else. The throughput is the energy taken into the system, which gets reorganized, and is referred to as work in the system. Energy comes into the system, and more energy is used to rearrange it into a product that will bring more energy into the system. The output is the resulting reorganization of energy and is exported into the environment as a product, service, or activity. Systems can appear as cycles of events whereby the foregoing cycle repeats itself as the output is used to obtain more energy to reorganize and export. Events create the structure, not things, and it's dynamically balancing itself rather than remaining static. But most important for our purposes in understanding the significance of failure are the features of information input, negative feedback, and the coding processes, whereby information input is nonenergic input that gives the system information about the environment and about how it functions in relation to the environment.

The crux of the relationship of the open system and failure is found in the role of negative feedback, which is observed in the system. Negative feedback is a type of information input that may come in the form or pain or failure. A thermostat reacts to negative feedback (falling temperature) and regulates the temperature of the room by signaling the furnace to act. If there is no way of taking in and using negative feedback, the system will expend too much energy or take in too much energy, upsetting the cycle, similar to leprosy, which disables the body's ability to feel pain. The body is unable to respond to extreme heat or pressure and sustains injury. A system is able to sort out the information that it needs and ignore the information that is irrelevant. The system thus reads and adjusts to the environment by what is called coding. According to this model, there is also the steady state and homeostasis, which is ever-changing and adjusting. Body temperature regulation is an example of the steady state. Disturbance in tissue will result in mobilization of energy to counter it. If this disturbance is repeated, the system will anticipate the disturbance and counter it before it happens. In the attempt to correct the system, organisms will over- or underreact, necessitating another reaction to maintain equilibrium. Since the system is open, there are always disturbances and adjustments being made. In humans too, it is important that there be space allowed to make such over- and underadjustments, in all facets of goal achievement from survival to ambition; those actions cannot be classified as failures.

Equifinality says there is no one best way to do things except under certain conditions, and these must be established before standardizing and repeating a method. As a result of trying to maintain stability, changes will occur in the system. Sometimes flexibility is what's needed, and coordination and control can become ends rather than means to the end. Irregularities from outside influences in the way a system works shouldn't be treated as error but incorporated into the analysis of your response. By assuming a closed system, the advantages of using feedback from outside the system may result in valuable corrections and adjustments being lost. These corrections are requisite elements to maintain balance within the system. Furthermore, failure and corrections in this way are the products of a corrective mechanism of the mind that enable us to make iterative adjustments on an ongoing basis. In short, *failure* and *correction* are somewhat synonymous whereby if we listen to what failure is telling us, we benefit from the feedback loop of failure coming into the system, and when we do not, it may be to our own detriment. Failure informs us that we need to adjust and correct and is a feature of the process of how we make it through life.

By understanding how we evolve within an environment and the role that trial and error or failure operates within the system of things, we can gain more control of our journey and gain a greater degree of emotional strength along the way. Adopting full control of our reactions and actions is a skill within itself. One way to practice is by reflection, resetting, and refocusing. Reflection brings clarity when seeking to understand ourselves. The open system spoken of above was originally developed by Ludwig von Bertanlanffy (1956) and defines a system as "an assemblage or combination of parts whose relations make them interdependent."

Throughout our lives, our psychological resilience is tested. We develop the ability to mentally or emotionally cope with a crisis at the earliest of ages. Developing behavioral capabilities that allow us to stay calm in any crisis is a healthful practice that is always worth putting time into. We all have good and bad days while going through our share of crises. Our initial reactions should not be our focus; however, our goal should be to bring that energy down with an aim of choosing to respond by remaining calm and rational because this is a healthier way of finding a solution to any challenging situation. Alternatively, responding with anger, fear, or any other negative emotion has a high probability of yielding a negative outcome for the main reason of operating from a stressful state. Once we understand our current selves thoroughly from our reactions to how and why we felt a certain way, then we can move forward, work toward better responses, and enjoy better outcomes. This is where we can start resetting with more knowledge and begin the process of starting again fresh.

Physiology of failure

The physiology of failure is particular to those specific processes responsible for our experiencing it in our bodies; what are the functions responsible for how we process it—physical, psychological, or otherwise? As we have seen, it may start as an idea associated with our collective survival and permeates through culture, thought, emotion, and ultimately, systems of action. Children conceive of the world through the eyes of their parents, inclusive of their self-image, character, personalities, beliefs, etc. In fact, it goes without saying that consistently negative or inconsistent experiences in childhood have an effect on how a child grows up. We experience failure in the same way through the eyes of our parents, culture, communities, etc. We may either develop a healthy relationship toward failing and become resilient and persevering in the face of adversity, or we may get frustrated, angry, and negative when challenged with something new that moves us outside our comfort zone and quit or give up as a result. However, exactly what determines how we will respond in each instance? How can we get the most out of our experiences with failure?

In order to interfere with the way a child sees and copes with the world, all you have to do as a parent is to fail to be predictable, rewarding, and consistently loving. Even prenatal toxic experiences by the mother can have detrimental long-term effects on the unborn child. Maternal anxiety and depression before childbirth predicts stress-related illness in offspring to a greater extent than would be expected. Anxiety is synonymous with vulnerability, and its origins can be tracked right back to childhood. A child must learn that he or she has control over what happens in their world by mastering the cause-and-effect nature of things. Otherwise, children will grow to believe that they have no influence on the world and that what they do just does not matter, being helpless in the face of seemingly random and chaotic events. It is this mental state that may lend itself to the child giving up and coping by quitting. No use in putting in effort when the outcomes are totally random. This learned helplessness makes the child vulnerable because its withdrawal from challenges, effort, social contact, or anything demanding, for that matter, makes them less able to learn skills, gain confidence, or build a meaningful life.

Another mechanism by which childhood adversity leads to increased vulnerability throughout life is in our "fight or flight" response to stress and anxiety, which is largely hormonal. It all comes down to the interplay between adrenaline—our short-term stress hormone that effectively gears us up for a fight to the death by increasing heart rate, breathing, blood pressure, the sensitivity of nerve endings, and the pattern of blood flow around the body—and cortisol—the body's long-term stress hormone that causes inflammatory processes, the metabolism to slow down, and the person to be less active. This hypothalamic-pituitary-adrenal (HPA) circuit (or axis)—which describes the interaction between the hypothalamus, pituitary gland, and adrenal glands—is programmed through childhood. If a child faces adversity through the first decade and a half of life, it will develop an HPA axis that is super sensitive, leading the child through life with a tendency to use fight-or-flight responses and the long-term effects of stress from stressful stimuli that others would normally react to with lower levels of stress. Prolonged or severe adverse events, especially early in life, reduce the levels of these chemicals in the pleasure/reward center, making it more difficult for a person to enjoy things and feel good in the future. Basically, childhood adversity makes you more vulnerable to quitting, giving up, and experiences of failure.

Take atychiphobia, for example, which is a fear of failure and may be part of another mood disorder, anxiety, or eating disorder. Phobias like atychiphobia can be so extreme that they completely paralyze you, making it difficult to carry on with your tasks at home, school, or work. You may even miss out on important opportunities in your life both personally and professionally. Self-handicapping is another possibility when you have this fear of failure; this means that you are so afraid of failing that you actually sabotage your efforts. For example, you may simply not start a big project for school, ultimately failing as a result. The idea here is that it's better to fail by not starting than by failing after putting in a lot of effort. In fact, this kind of fear may occur not because we are afraid of the effort but because we are afraid of what happens next after we make the effort and fall short. The death of the dream itself can be unbearable because where do you go afterward? How do you recover from that: after you have written the book, after you've applied to the program, after you've played in the recital, etc., which was an integral step to achieving the dream, you bombed? Rather than living with the dream deferred with all of its anticipation, expectancy, and excitement around what-ifs, we now have closure that it will never happen for us. Most of the excitement around holding a lottery ticket is in the dream of winning, the act of gambling, and all the promise that it holds for the happiness to follow after the win. It's the anticipation that keeps us running and the realization or fear of losing that sometimes keeps us from even checking the whether we won or lost. This can be a crushing realization that you will never be a champion boxer, astronaut, entrepreneur, etc. Isn't it better to live with the what-if excitement of the dream while never materializing the reality of your failing to achieve it? This problem is, like the lottery, you have got to be in it to win it. You can't win if you don't play, and playing with the knowledge that you may fail takes courage and emotional strength, among other things. It's important to accept the inevitability of failing and falling short in order to handle what's next in the journey to your aspirations.

How can we gain strength and overcome learned helplessness and the propensity to quit in the face of fear or falling short? The way forward lies in understanding that even in failure, there is much to be learned and strength to be gained. In fact, Jack Foster, author of *How to Get Ideas*, based on his personal account of the NASA selection process for astronauts, noted that a person who had failed and got up again was a stronger contender than one who had never experienced failure. Similarly, Dr. Brene Brown, in the YouTube documentary

The Call to Courage, recited an excerpt from one of Teddy Roosevelt's speeches, stating that

> *It's not the critic who counts; not the man who points out how the strong man stumble, or where the doer of deeds could have done them better. The credit belongs to the man who is actually in the arena, whose face is marred by dust and sweat and blood, who strives valiantly; who errs and without error and shortcomings; but who does actively strive to do the deed; who knows the great enthusiasm, the great devotions, who spends himself in a worthy cause, who at the best knows in the end the triumph of high achievement and who at the worst, if he fails, at least he fails while daring greatly.*

Dr. Brown goes on to point out that winning is sometimes showing up and losing rather than running away and that in order to innovate, you must be prepared to fail. She analogizes courage to an openness to falling short of one's goals or failure in order to reap the benefits of eventual success. According to Dr. Brown, courage is seeking something real, durable, and valuable, and you can only find that by putting the real you out there, being intimate enough to let yourself be hurt. In order to discover things, gain wisdom, and create anything original, you have to be prepared to be wrong. In fact, we must beware of anyone who is too certain about anything, particularly if he is critical of anyone not sharing his belief. The chances are he has never thought deeply enough or let himself be vulnerable enough to learn anything real from his life. According to "Cantopher's Law," the degree of a person's certainty is inversely proportional to his or her wisdom. Inspiration for Cantopher's Law can be seen illustrated in a painting, referred to as *Christ Mocked*, or Bosch's painting, *Christ Crowned with Thorns*.

According to Terry Winograd and Fernando Flores (1990) the great temptations, as depicted in the painting, suggest a universal sense of evil contrasted with the kingdom of heaven. Christ in the center expresses the utmost patience and acceptance with his tormentors on each side, shown as four human figures that represent a total view of humanity. The author's observed that each human type is like a great temptation against the expansiveness and patience of Christ's expression, pointing out that they represent four styles of estrangement and loss of interior calm. The figure in the lower right of the painting is grabbing Jesus by the robe and tugging him to the ground. He holds on to him and restricts his freedom, fastening his attention on Jesus. He seems to be telling him, "Now listen to me. I know what I am saying!" This is the temptation of certainty. We tend to live in a world of certainty, a Cartesian reality where our convictions prove that things are the way we see them and that there is no alternative to what we hold as true. This is our daily situation, our cultural condition, and our common way of being human. The real issue or problem that comes with certainty is that we must free our mind to challenge our perspective; otherwise, it may be our very perspective that blocks our creativity as it shapes our perceptions. We get used to seeing things through a filter of our biases, past learnings, and cultural traditions. People with strong perceptual sets are prone to being seduced by certainty, culminating in quick decision-making and jumping to conclusions as they require answers over processing and understanding. They don't seek alternatives because they think that their perspective is the only one that matters and that they will become limited from seeking other perceptions on any given situation. Oftentimes we require different perspectives on our situation in order to get a different perception, and certainty blinds us to such alternatives as it tends to lock us into our perspective. Often, this is the case—that there is more to be seen in what we think we see.

We must refrain from the habit of falling into the temptation of certainty. This is necessary for two reasons. On the one hand, if the reader does not suspend his or her certainties, they cannot communicate anything here, which will be embodied in his or her experience, as an effective understanding of the phenomenon of cognition. On the other hand, they seek to lead the reader to scrutinize the phenomenon of cognition, and our actions flowing from it is because all cognitive experience involves the knower in a personal way, rooted in his biological structure. There, his experience of certainty is an individual phenomenon, blind to the cognitive acts of others, in a solitude that is transcended only in a world created with those others. A great example of this comes by way of a recent article about four famous philosophers who realized they were completely wrong. While most philosophers make minor adjustments to their arguments to correct mistakes, these four made large shifts in their thinking. In fact, illustrating the notion that in one's pursuit to discovery and wisdom and to create anything original, you have to be prepared to be wrong, these four philosophers went back on what they said earlier in often radical ways—a journey that can be impeded by certainty.

The first is Robert Nozick, an American philosopher who wrote on every subject he could get his hands on. He is well known for his lone venture into political philosophy—anarchy, state, and utopia, where he argues for a minimalist state that never infringes on personal liberties. At one point, he even muses over how an income tax is akin to part-time slavery as a worker is paid in wages, and a part of them are given to the state without the chance to opt out. His ideal state wouldn't have any taxation. In his later book *The Examined Life*, Nozick reflects on his earlier book and declares, "The libertarian position I once propended now seems to me seriously inadequate, in part because it did not fully knit the humane considerations and joint cooperative activities it left room for more closely into its fabric." Although he doesn't fundamentally change his position, he does admit to problems with it. He endorses the idea that the state can ban discrimination against various groups, admits that the realization of personal freedom may require mandated group effort, and yields to the use of taxation or mandated donation to specific charities as a means to assure society continues to function. While in later interviews, he assured readers that he had not abandoned libertarianism, but he did take the edge off a few of the more hard-lined views as he aged.

The second is Ludwig Wittgenstein, an Austrian philosopher in the twentieth century who published a single book during his lifetime, the *Tractatus Logico-Philosophicus*. His was perhaps the most radical turnaround among the group. In his book, he argues that when we are communicating with another person, we are using words to put pictures in their minds. Wittgenstein was rather proud of his book and was convinced that he had solved philosophy with it by reducing all problems to semantics. He retired from writing for a few years as there was no more philosophy to do. He later changed his mind about that. In his other book, the one published after his death, *Philosophical Investigations*, he wrote, "The author of the *Tractatus* was mistaken," as he had moved so far away from his original positions.

The third, Jean-Paul Sartre, one of the leading minds behind existentialism in the twentieth century, had reversed course as well. He wrote numerous books, essays, and plays describing his way of thinking and how we could learn from it. In his earliest works, Sartre introduces us to the idea of our absolute freedom. While he admits that we are limited by some physical and social circumstances, he places us utterly in charge of ourselves and declares us "condemned to be free." While he always admitted that social, economic, and physical limits to our freedom existed, the limits he acknowledged became more numerous and restricting over time. This was due, in part, to the influence of his life partner Simone de Beauvoir and his increasing association with the French left. His changes are less of a radical turnaround in his thinking and more of an evolution in his understanding of the practical side of his work.

Lastly, there was Jean Meslier, who was a Catholic priest in seventeenth-century France. Noted as a quiet, dependable, and unremarkable priest, he served his parish for over forty years without complaint. After his death, a six-hundred-plus-page book promoting atheism was found in his room. It has been published as *Testament*. Reverend Meslier has the distinction of being the first atheist philosopher to write a text defending his position. In it, he describes all religion as "a castle in the air" and theology as "but ignorance of natural causes reduced to a system." He found the problem of evil to be unsolvable, denied the existence of free will and the soul, and stated that the nobility and priests deserved to be slaughtered in the name of truth and justice. He also makes the argument that Christianity, as it existed at the time, was merely a tool to assure the passivity of the lower classes against injustices they should be revolting against. He advocated for a protocommunism as a solution to social injustice. While the question of how much of a turnaround this constitutes is unknowable, he admitted in his text that he entered the seminary to please his parents. It does stand against his forty years of preaching Christianity. Nobody else on this list denounced forty years of work in a single book, and his rejection of it comes with a force that stands out despite his cumbersome writing style.

As strivers, we must maintain an open mind and a humble disposition, or we become closed to the realm of infinite possibilities. Most of us know that we don't know everything but also harbor the belief that we know all we need to know that is germane to our present life condition. However, the reality is that we don't know enough to even make such a statement or harbor such a belief. How, then, can we grow and come into new spaces of new opportunities and possibilities that move us in entirely new directions? The minute we assume that we know all we need to know is the minute we shut down the infinite possibilities in the universe that await us as we stop searching for creative solutions. We become pragmatic, stiff, and rigid as we lose our imagination, our ability to dream, and the childlike mood of wonder. We must foster and maintain a degree of humility that affords us the flexibility to not only know that we don't know all we need to know but also allows us to know and accept when we are wrong and allows us the desire to make necessary changes in our perspective when warranted. Just as with our four philosophers and what so many others have done en route to achieving great things, we must resist the temptation of certainty and embrace humility in the face of failure in order to learn from it. What follows in the next section is a broader discussion of the virtues of failure and their significance in aiding our understanding of the power of failure and falling short. This is followed by a series of brief case studies of individuals who experienced significant failures that fueled a subsequent rise to great success in their chosen fields, and a summary of principles of failure that laid the foundations for their respective successes.

2

VIRTUES OF FAILURE

Failure is a great teacher and, if you are open to
it, every mistake has a lesson to offer.

—Oprah Winfrey

Unfortunately, it's a great disservice to everyone, especially young people, that the stories that we often hear about the most accomplished public figures sound so effortless when, in fact, they came at a great cost even for visionary-creative success stories like those of Mark Zuckerberg, Jack Dorsey, Howard Schultz, Wendy Kopp, and even the legendary Steve Jobs. It took Dorsey years of experimentation before he finally latched on to what ultimately became Twitter. Wendy Kopp started Teach for America initially as a conference and on a shoestring budget after graduating from college.

And Howard Schultz, while he had great foresight to recognize that Americans needed a communal coffee experience like those that existed in Europe, failed on his first try. As was written in *Little Bets* by Peter Sims, when his first store opened in Seattle in 1986, there was nonstop opera music, menus in Italian, and no chairs. As Schultz acknowledged, he and his colleagues had to make a lot of mistakes to discover what would become the Starbucks we know today.

Marcus Aurelius once stated that "our actions may be impeded… but there can be no impeding our intentions or dispositions. Because we can accommodate and adapt. The mind adapts and converts to its own purposes the obstacle to our acting…the impediment to action advances action. What stands in the way becomes the way." Aurelius was talking about turning obstacles into opportunities and squeezing victories from failures. Aurelius highlights that setbacks and problems are always to be expected and are never permanent, and he makes certain that what impedes us can only empower us. What doesn't kill us only makes us stronger. What the emperor saw was that hidden within each and every obstacle often lies an opportunity to practice some virtue: patience, courage, humility, resourcefulness, reason, justice, and creativity.

These are the lessons that I learned from failure.

Failure is the foundation of success

We are all familiar with the phrases "No pain, no gain" and "Feel the burn"; you are if you hang out in the gym as much as I do anyway. What do these phrases really mean beyond the commercialized references, and what does it have to do with the virtues of failure, for that matter? Well, scientifically speaking, skeletal muscle is composed of threadlike myofibrils and sarcomeres that form a muscle fiber and are the basic units of contraction. The 650 skeletal muscles in the human body contract when they receive signals from motor neurons, which are triggered from a part of the cell called the sarcoplasmic reticulum. Motor neurons (in our brain) tell muscles when to contract, and the better you are at heeding these signals the stronger you can get in terms of physical power/muscle contraction. After a workout, the body repairs or replaces damaged muscle fibers through a cellular process where it fuses these fibers together to form new muscle protein strands or myofibrils. These repaired muscles increase in thickness and number to create muscle hypertrophy or growth. While we are at rest, muscle growth occurs whenever the rate of muscle protein synthesis is greater than the rate of muscle protein breakdown. Satellite cells act like stem cells for the muscles and add up to existing muscle mass. When activated, they help add more nuclei to the muscle cells and therefore contribute directly to the growth of muscle tissue. As these processes occur, our muscles expend lactic acid, and while we are at rest, it pools in the joints mostly and creates an intense burning sensation. This is confirmation that the foregoing processes are at work and is evidence of a fruitful workout. Bodybuilders actually seek out this pain, this breaking down of the cells. They seek to "suffer" just to know that the growth is happening. No pain, no gain. In fact, there is no growth without the burn, without the pain—without the breaking down and recovery. The principle is the same in life: the pain cannot be avoided (should not be avoided) on our way to excellence in any endeavor; the breaking down to build oneself up is a necessary element of the journey.

As parents, it is important to fail and even more important to give our children permission to fail, letting them learn early that surviving defeat makes you tougher and more resilient for the rest of your life and that only by risking failure are we likely to accomplish anything. Michael Jordan once recalled that he had missed more than nine thousand shots in his career, stating, "I have lost almost three hundred games, and twenty-six times, I've been trusted to take the game-winning shot and missed. I failed over and over and over again in my life, and that is why I succeed." There is no accomplishment without risk. Failure gives us a unique opportunity to learn. It's no accident that Harvard Business School students study unsuccessful companies. Success is enjoyable, but there is very little to learn from it. Probably the one area of American life where failure is regarded positively is science. Unlike the world of business, sports politics, and academics, science understands failure for what it is: the outcome to an event, the result of an experiment, and a chance to correct mistakes and move on to grow from them.

In a recent commencement address to the University of Pennsylvania, Denzel Washington noted that baseball legend Reggie Jackson struck out 2,600 times in his career—the most in the history of baseball, but you don't hear about the strike-outs, only what made him great. Thomas Edison, in his invention of the light bulb, made over a thousand versions of the incandescent light bulb, as evidenced by the number of patents submitted before stumbling across the one that would maintain light. Washington mentions about his own acting career, saying, "If you hang around the barbershop long enough, you're eventually going to get a haircut." Speaking of the number of times he himself experienced failures to secure roles and his resilience to keep coming back, his big break finally came in a play called *Fences* on

Broadway. The play won a Tony Award; however, Washington noted the irony that the play opened at the Cort Theatre, which is where he suffered his greatest rejection years earlier. Les Brown, the motivational speaker, wants us to consider what to say to our many anthropomorphized ideas on our deathbed, asking, "Imagine you're on your deathbed, and standing around you are the ghosts of the ideas you've never acted on. The ghosts are angry, disappointed, and upset. They say, 'We came to you because you could've brought us to life, and now we have to go to the grave together.'" TD Jakes, in an interview called "Invest in Yourself When You Are Failing," said that in everything he did, he failed at least once. He tells a story of how his early forays into theater were futile as he went bankrupt because he failed to sell enough tickets to break even on the first play, stating that central to the art of being an entrepreneur is investing in yourself when you're failing. He also asserted that you have to keep investing in yourself even though things are not working in order to get it done. Bishop Jakes didn't look at failure as failure but failure as education, and that education always comes with a tuition—the price paid for the learning. Wisdom gained from his early mistakes led Bishop Jakes to partner with Tyler Perry, who, at a time, was practically homeless. Tyler Perry had figured out how to be profitable in the theater business, so Bishop Jakes thought, *Why recreate the wheel?* So they got together to put the play on tour. Their screenwriter at the time, Ruben Kannan, then made a movie out of it. Originally considered for television, it was supposed to be for theater. But Kannan entered the movie in the Santa Barbara Film Festival, and they won the film festival. Bishop Jakes recalls that they took a movie that was meant to be on TV, and it ended up on 403 screens across America. But people think, *All you do is win.*

There are numerous losses along the way that educate us and make us stronger for the win. However, if you didn't fail, you would not be tough enough to handle all that comes with winning. In fact, we should be more thankful for our failures than for the winnings because when everything goes right, it may make us spoiled children, and spoiled children can't take tough times. We cannot be afraid of tough times because we all experience tough times. It's the tough times that give us options. Whenever confronted with failure—unless you choose to do nothing—the result of your actions will always be change (e.g., you have either met new people, come to some resolution, etc.). Failure will give you many more options than a successful venture would have given. Elon Musk stated that one of the most difficult choices he's had to face in life was in 2008. He hadn't had not much money in the bank at the time and was presented with two investment choices: (one) put all available funds into one company and then let his other company die or (two) split the funds between the two companies, but then they both might die. Musk stated,

When you put sweat and tears into creating something, it's like your children, and you are asking yourself, "Which one am I going to let starve to death?" So I split the money between two. My biggest failure was SpaceX. With the first three launches being failures, we were actually just barely able to scrape together enough parts and money to do the fourth launch. If the fourth launch failed, we would have been dead. However, there were multiple failures along the way, and I tried very hard to get the right expertise in for SpaceX. I tried hard to find a great chief engineer for the rocket. But good chief engineers would not join, and the bad ones, there's no point hiring them. So I ended up being the chief engineer. If I could have found somebody better, maybe I would have had less than three failures.

When asked whether after that third failure in a row should he have packed it in, he said, "No, I don't ever give up." Elon Musk has been referred to the real-life Iron Man; he is a cofounder and CEO of Tesla, CEO of SpaceX, cofounder of Neuralink, founder of PayPal, and cofounder of OpenAI. According to *Forbes*, he is the twentieth richest person in the world with a net worth of about 30.1 billion dollars.

Self-awareness

Terry Winograd and Fernando Flores (1990) once wrote that the "moment of reflection before a mirror is always a peculiar moment: it is the moment when we become aware of that part of ourselves which we cannot see in any other way—as when we reveal the blind spot that shows us our own structure, as when we suppress the blindness that it entails filling the blank space. That reflection is an act of turning back upon ourselves. It is the only chance we have to discover our blindness." This is a fitting observation to begin any discussion on self-awareness. What these authors are simply stating is the difficulty involved in being an observer of ourselves. If we are to autocorrect failures in our lives, we must see where we fall short in our awareness from each direction, especially those that we are blind to. One saving grace to address this issue can be found in our networks of friends, family, and colleagues that we develop over time. Solipsism asserts that we exist only in the eyes of each other; apparently, the "other" may provide this missing source of self-reflection through which we may become more self-aware. This view is opposed to the objective, or Cartesian, view of reality, where we all live in a fixed and knowable world. Solipsism is kind of like in the *Matrix* movies with Keanu Reeves, where only what you imagine to be real is real. To acquire self-awareness of any given situation is no simple task, but with the thoughts, opinions, and ideas of these networks of love, professional help, and support, we can become better at capturing and correcting those blind spots.

The very idea of a situation means that we are not standing outside it (and, in fact, are part of it) and hence are unable to have any objective knowledge of it. Much like a fish in water who cannot see the water it's in, it's only when the fish is removed from the water that it becomes aware of the water. Like the fish, we are always within the situation, and to throw light on it is a task that is never entirely completed. This is true as we can become aware of some of our prejudices and, in that way, emancipate ourselves from some of the limits they place on our thinking, but we commit a fallacy in believing we can ever be free of all prejudice. In fact, most of what you see is an illusion. Our eyes aren't all-seeing but capture fleeting glimpses of the outside world between rapid movements called "saccades". During these episodes, we are effectively blind because the brain doesn't process the information that comes in when they happen. The brain, after all, is sealed in darkness and silence within the solid casing of the skull. It has no direct access to the outside world, and so it relies on the information that reaches it via a few electrical cables from our sensory organs. Our eyes pick up information about wavelengths of electromagnetic radiation, our ears detect vibrations of air particles, and our noses and mouths detect volatile molecules that we experience as smells and flavors. Through complex processes we only partly understand, the brain integrates these independent inputs into a unified conscious awareness. If you believe that reality is something that is inherently different from the mind, then it becomes paradoxical to think that we've ever have access to reality. Reality depends on us; it depends on the way we see the world. But at the same time, what we're perceiving is one aspect of this reality because our perception is shaped by the senses we happen to have.

"But why all this talk of the nature of reality? I thought this was about self-awareness and failure." Recovering from failure requires a clear view of oneself and the nature of the shortcoming. Only then can you correct in the next instance. It follows, then, that we are responsible for who we are and what we become; it's not to be left up to others as our public identity is very important in the pursuit of self-awareness. The key takeaway here is that we are what we say we are and not what others call us! In a 2019 article on self-awareness, Bijay Maharjan asks, "How do you react and what is your emotional state when you fail?" His article presents a brief discussion about the various dimensions of failure and how to use our self-awareness to learn from failures. He provides three situations that will happen as soon as people fail, which define three kinds of people at the same time:

- Indifference to the failure
- Pain/blaming/giving up
- Pain/self-awareness

The indifferent people are so careless with their life that any failure they experience will make no difference to them as if nothing has happened. They simply walk away and start the same work all over again with no sense of improvement. This, unfortunately, is their habit as they continue to make the same mistakes over and over, and as a result, they will always be in the middle of nowhere.

The pain/blaming/giving-up folks, when confronted by failure, will go through so much anxiety, tension, and regret, that they will start blaming others for the failure. Some examples would be these: During a USA student visa interview, they may claim the questions were too tough, that the interviewer had an attitude with them, or that they were actually physically sick at that moment; or even when they fail an exam, they would say that the study environment at home was just not conducive, that the questions were biased, or that they were just unlucky. And when they fail at relationships, they will say, "I just picked the wrong one," "Her or his behavior is not suitable for me," etc. When they fail in the workplace, they will say, "My boss had it in for me," "The job sucks," "The management system is the worst," "My teammates don't have the proper credentials," and the list goes on. After this, they will have a feeling of giving up the work or task they were doing because they can't face the consequences of failure, and they feel completely helpless to influence change in their lives.

The pain/self-awareness, people however, go through pain, feel down, experience anxiety, and worry. But such feelings will not stay long for them. They will sit down, center and ground themselves, settle their mind, and start thinking, *Where did I go wrong?* This only after they did all they could have done, given the circumstances. Here self-awareness plays a significant role to tackle failure. Self-awareness is about asking questions of yourself and telling or commanding things to be so. Let's use a workplace for an example. Consider you have a quarterly performance measurement system in your organization, and you fail to meet a basic standard of your position. You will construct a narrative or story in your mind to make sense of why you fell short. Perhaps a story of last quarter comes to you, and instantly your mind replays your strengths, weaknesses, opportunities, and threats. This way, you can find out what were the obstacles and challenges that prohibited you from meeting your performance target. Maybe your working style was not suitable, and you got distracted. Maybe your focus was on the wrong target. Maybe you didn't care at the beginning and didn't have enough time to make a solid showing at the end. Here, in this mindset, you can ask questions like "Why couldn't I achieve this target?" "What were weak points?" and "Which part did I fail to address?" And now the second part of self-awareness is telling yourself after knowing your weak points something like, "From now on, you will focus on the target. You will have a deeper understanding of tactics to employ, and you will use best working style that is required. You will be more diligent about your time, and you will seek to improve your team members' contributions." This way, this failure can be addressed with self-awareness. This way, we can exploit options made available in our failings and can get more out of the experience.

Self-awareness is easier said than done when trying to achieve it. How exactly does one go about securing an objective view of oneself, let alone maintaining a clear vision as to why and where we may be failing? Clearly, if we could be perfect observers of ourselves, we could fix everything before the realization of negative consequences set in. The Johari window is one method of achieving an objective view of our failures through the eyes of the other. The Johari window is a technique that helps people better understand their relationship with themselves and others. It was created by psychologists Joseph Luft (1916–2014) and Harrington Ingham (1916–1995) in 1955 and is used primarily in self-help groups and corporate settings as a heuristic exercise. The name Johari comes from when the creators Joseph Luft and Anne Harrington Ingram took the first letters of their names and combined them to make the name of the model. The Johari window provides a way to increase our self-perception.

The Johari window is a two-by-two model that is illustrated by four squares or windows in the form of a matrix. Within these windows, along the X axis, is both what we know about ourselves and

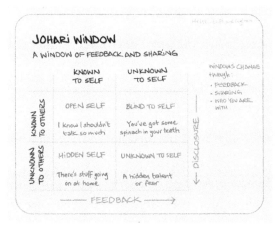

don't know about ourselves, and along the *Y* axis, we have what's known to others and not known to others about us. And that gives us four squares. Each square may differ in size, depending upon the individual, and it all depends on how well you know yourself and how well others know you. Starting with the most obvious of the four windows, this represents everything we know about ourselves and everything that others know about us. This window is called the open area or arena. Some describe this as the "I know you know" window. The second window is called the hidden area; this is sometimes called the facade window or the masked window. The phrase that describes this window is "I know, but you don't." The information here is private, or under wraps, like your fears or other issues. The third window is called the blind area or blind spot and is most significant for our purposes here among the virtues of failure. The phrase that describes this window is "I don't know, but you do." It's not enough to make subjective assessments about what is already obvious to ourselves about ourselves without an ability to view ourselves objectively (i.e., without understanding our blind areas). This information can be in the form of body language, habits, mannerisms, tone of voice, etc. Our blind spots are the things that we are not aware of and involve exposing weaknesses and imperfections, which can also be exploited by other people. The Johari Window, specifically the blind spot, is incorporated here among the virtues of failure to demonstrate that as much as failure is largely a subjective assessment, it may also appear as an objective assessment with real-world consequences even though we may not be aware of its existence and application to us. Although we may not be aware of certain things about ourselves, others are. The key purpose of this square is so that you can use it to figure out what other people think to help you grow. So your friends, for example, can help you mature if you're open to feedback about what they see in you. Emphasis on "help you grow," which requires feedback, negative as well as positive, such that by virtue of enhanced self-awareness, we may correct our course and stay on track. What this demonstrates is the importance of uncovering your blind spot such that you may increase your self-awareness, enabling greater self-reflection and insight, which in turn allows you to get the most out of corrective situations. As with open systems discussed earlier, such feedback is crucial in making such determinations and getting the most out of the lessons inherent in failure. The fourth square is the unknown, and the phrase for this is "I don't know, and you don't know." The paradox to this one is if nobody knows, at least not yet, the question is, "How do we know this square even exists?" Well, we know this information is there, waiting to be discovered, because in the past, when we have had new experiences, we have learned more about who we are that we previously did not know ("Failure Is Not the End of Your Story", YouTube compilation, accessed June 21, 2021).

The long and the short of it is that making grounded assessments of our shortcomings is crucial to our ability to correct mistakes and failings. This is very difficult to almost impossible when we cannot adequately and objectively observe ourselves. We never really know how we appear to others, nor do we know if they truly understand what we are trying to say. The goal of the Johari window is to expand the shared area without abandoning information that is strictly personal. Shrinking the blind zone is a win-win situation. The individual gains valuable insight by learning from his colleagues. Sharing information improves overall team performance and engagement. Indeed, when team members know each other, they build a bond of trust—

an environment where everyone readily exchanges ideas and quickly develops optimal business and social relationships. Conversely, if trust is low, teams compensate with political games, wasting everyone's time and undermining both morale and performance. In extreme cases, low trust breeds a desire for revenge—the ultimate destroyer of personal and material value. It is even possible to shrink the unknown zone by sharing information and making sense of why we behave in certain ways. This is a joint discovery and is made easier by having more than one set of eyes looking at your beliefs and behavior. The Johari window is an elegant tool for self-realization, allowing us to work with others to discover our strengths and weaknesses and to see ourselves as others see us.

Special note on race, gender, and implicit bias in being self-aware

We are all familiar with the saying "If you are white, you are right. If you are brown, stick around. If you are black, get back." Basically, this invokes the idea that there exists a cultural bias with respect to inclusion on all things social, economic, and in many instances, legal on the basis of your color and or nationality. Like racism, this heuristic permeates in all aspects of our lives including perceptions about your public identity, which points to the value of your contributions based on race. This goes to the earlier point about objective negative ungrounded assessments of failure that may have had an impact on your sense of self-awareness. What do we do when trying to learn and understand from assessments of failure in an attempt to better ourselves when such judgements are tainted through a lens of cultural and racial bias of others? As the Johari window talks about objective assessments of failure as viewed from the perspective of others, it leaves us to think that sometimes, when others are different, they can be assessed unfairly as a failure when really, the seemingly objective observation is more about the person's cultural, racial, or gender differences than the fact that they're doing something inconsistent with the proper way that it should be done. This is tantamount to nothing more than a distortion, which may undermine our collective self-image and self-awareness—much like being forced to look into a broken mirror that reflects a self that is not exactly reflective of the self that you are being in that moment. Such observations lead me to discuss this special note on implicit bias, as race is the most prominent difference among us whereby people can mistakenly be charged as failures.

Case in point is a recent statement by Larry Summers when he was president of Harvard University and provoked a furor by arguing that men outperform women in math and sciences because of biological difference and that discrimination is no longer a career barrier for female academics. Lawrence Summers, a career economist who served as treasury secretary under President Clinton, has a reputation for outspokenness. He made his remarks at a private conference on the position of women and minorities in science and engineering, hosted by the National Bureau of Economic Research. In a lengthy address delivered without notes, Dr. Summers offered three explanations for the shortage of women in senior posts in science and engineering, starting with their reluctance to work long hours because of childcare responsibilities. Early in his speech, Summers noted that women remain underrepresented in the upper echelons of academic and professional life in part, he said, because many women with young children are unwilling or unable to put in the eighty-hour workweeks needed to succeed in those fields. He went on to argue that boys outperform girls on high school science and math scores because of genetic differences. According to Summers, "Research in behavioral genetics is showing that things people previously attributed to socialization weren't due to socialization after all."

As an example, Summers told the conference about giving his daughter two trucks. She treated them like dolls and named them mommy and daddy trucks, he said. Dr. Summers also played down the impact of sex bias in appointments to academic institutions. He said, "The real issue is the overall size of the pool, and it's less clear how much the size of the pool was held down by discrimination." At least half of his audience was comprised of women. Several said they found the remarks offensive, and one walked out. During Dr. Summers's presidency, the number of tenured jobs offered to women had fallen from 36 percent to 13 percent whereas only four of thirty-two tenured job openings were offered to women. How much of what Dr. Summers says is more tied to social roles and expectations, the economic structure of a society that expects stay-at-home-parents in order to function properly, and cultural biases that reinforce gender roles than is actually capable of whether it be a woman or not? And it is just such ungrounded negative assessment on which we form the basis of our self-worth, contributions, successes, and failures on.

Similarly, in a now infamous interview with WRC-TV's Ed Hotaling for a program on the birthday of Martin Luther King Jr., Jimmy "the Greek" Snyder, a popular New York City sportscaster, made a number of remarks about Black and White athletes, which had patently racist overtones and touched off a storm of protests across the country from viewers, television and radio commentators, and some Black leaders. Some of the statements Snyder made in the interview included, "The Black is a better athlete to begin with because he's been bred that way, because of his high thighs that go up into his back. And they can jump higher and run faster because of their bigger thighs." Snyder continued, "This all goes back to the Civil War, when, during the slave trading, the slave owner would breed his big Black to his big woman so that he would have a big Black kid. That's where it all started." The issue here is that it implies Blacks have not worked for what they have achieved and that their success on the field is largely due to the White man at the end of the day, as with everything else, for that matter, among other things. Even more insidious is the concept that Blacks are somehow not responsible for what they have become and that their success is due to some kind of unfair advantage. They are not even allowed to excel in sports, let alone anywhere else. What makes it insidious is the way in which such prejudiced and discriminatory beliefs held and imposed by society on a group create a feeling of inferiority among the group, damaging their self-esteem.

Illustrating the damage to one's sense of self was a study done by Rosenthal and Jacobsen in 1968 called the Pygmalion effect or Rosenthal effect, which is a psychological phenomenon wherein high expectations lead to improved performance in a given area while low expectations lead to worse. The effect is named after the Greek myth of Pygmalion, a sculptor who fell in love with a statue he had carved. Rosenthal and Jacobson applied the idea to teachers' expectations of their students affecting the students' performance. The idea was to figure out what would happen if teachers were told that certain kids in their class were destined to succeed, so Rosenthal took a normal IQ test and dressed it up as a different test. Rosenthal told the teachers that this very special test from Harvard had the very special ability to predict which kids were about to be very special—that is, which kids were about to experience a dramatic growth in their IQ. After the kids took the test, he then chose from every class several children totally at random. There was nothing at all to distinguish these kids from the other kids, but he told their teachers that the test predicted the kids were on the verge of an intense intellectual bloom. Rosenthal and Jacobson held that although high expectations lead to better performance and low expectations lead to worse, both effects lead to self-fulfilling prophecy. They believed that even attitude or mood could positively affect the students when the teacher was made aware of the "bloomers." Rosenthal predicted that elementary school teachers may subconsciously behave in ways that facilitate and encourage the students' success.

According to the Pygmalion effect, the targets of the expectations internalize their positive labels, and those with positive labels succeed accordingly. A similar process works in the opposite direction in the case of low expectations. The idea behind the Pygmalion effect is that increasing the leader's expectation of the follower's performance will result in better follower performance. Within sociology, the effect is often cited with regard to education and social class. This study supported the hypothesis that reality can be positively or negatively influenced by the expectations of others, called the observer-expectancy effect. Rosenthal argued that biased expectancies could affect reality and create self-fulfilling prophecies. But just how do expectations influence IQ? As Rosenthal did more research, he found that expectations affect teachers' moment-to-moment interactions with the children they teach in a thousand almost invisible ways. Teachers give the students that they expect to succeed more time to answer questions, more specific feedback, and more approval. They consistently touch, nod, and smile at those kids more. "It's not magic, it's not mental telepathy," Rosenthal says. "It's very likely these thousands of different ways of treating people in small ways every day."

Then there was the Significance Doll Test. In the 1940s, psychologists Kenneth and Mamie Clark designed and conducted a series of experiments known colloquially as the doll tests to study the psychological effects of segregation on African American children. Drs. Clark used four dolls identical except for color to test children's racial perceptions. Their subjects, children between the ages of three to seven, were asked to identify both the race of the dolls and which color doll they prefer. A majority of the children preferred the white doll and assigned positive characteristics to it. The Clarks concluded that prejudice, discrimination, and segregation created a feeling of inferiority among African American children and damaged their self-esteem. In an interview on the award-winning PBS documentary of the Civil Rights movement *Eyes on the Prize*, Dr. Kenneth Clark recalled, "The dolls test was an attempt on the part of my wife and me to study the development of the sense of self-esteem in children. We worked with Black children to see the extent to which their color, their sense of their own race and status, influenced their judgment about themselves, self-esteem." Drs. Clark stated that they did it to communicate to their colleagues in psychology the influence of race, color, and status on the self-esteem of children. In a particularly memorable episode, while Dr. Clark was conducting experiments in rural Arkansas, he asked a Black child which doll was most like him. The child responded while smiling and pointing to the brown doll, "That's a nigger. I'm a nigger." Dr. Clark described this experience as "disturbing, or more disturbing, than the children in Massachusetts who would refuse to answer the question or who would cry and run out of the room."

In 2014, research conducted by the Nextion leadership consulting firm revealed the unconscious racial bias we all carry with us among the legal profession even when we're supposedly using objective criteria like how many spelling errors an employee makes. In "Written in Black and White," selected law firm partners were asked to evaluate a single research memo into which twenty-two different errors were deliberately inserted: seven spelling/grammar errors, six substantive writing errors, five errors in fact, and four analytic errors. Half of the partner evaluators were told that the hypothetical associate author was African American, and half were told that the author was Caucasian. On a five-point scale, reviews for the exact same memo averaged a 3.2 for the African American author and 4.1 for the Caucasian author. More surprising were the findings of "objective" criteria such as spelling. The partner evaluators found an average of 2.9 spelling and grammar errors for the Caucasian authors and 5.8 such errors for the African American authors. Fewer technical writing and factual errors were also found in the memo by the supposedly White writer, though the disparity wasn't as great. Overall, the memo presumed to have been written by a Caucasian was "evaluated to be better in regards to the analysis of facts and had substantively fewer critical comments." The reviewers gave the memo supposedly written by a White man a rating of 4.1 out of five while they gave the memo supposedly written by a Black man a rating of 3.2 out of five. The White Thomas Meyer was praised for his potential and good analytical skills while the Black Thomas Meyer was criticized as average at best and needing a lot of work.

Lastly, in another study by McNiel (2017), in her master's thesis, "The Development of Consciousness in Negro Preschool Children," she surveyed 150 Black preschool-aged boys and girls from a DC nursery school to explore issues of race and child development—specifically the age at which Black children become aware that they are Black. For the study that formed the basis of her thesis, she and her husband, Kenneth, recruited the children and presented them with a set of pictures: White boys, Black boys, and benign images of animals and other objects. They asked the boys to pick which picture looked like them and then asked the girls to pick which picture looked like their brother or other male relative. The conclusion of the study showed a distinct racial awareness of self in boys aged three to four years old. The results were, in Kenneth's words, yet again, disturbing.

What we learn from these studies is that oftentimes, ungrounded negative assessments can be embedded in concepts, beliefs, biases, and predisposed notions on the basis of race and gender, which not only have anything to do with one's actual capability or intellect but lend to assessments of value in light of the success and failure of an individual as determined by others in our community. The ungrounded negative assessments are recursive in nature and self-reinforcing on the individual's self-image, undermining their belief in themselves. Relying on these assessments to understand your value within the community obviously can be detrimental to your sense of worth and the value of your contribution. In certain circumstances, we must proceed with caution. Unexamined adherence to statements from the likes of Dr. Summers and Jimmy the Greek may lead you to mischaracterize self-reflection, discounting your worth, value, and contributions and even viewing your actions and efforts as mistakes or even ungrounded judgments of failure simply by virtue of being a woman or not White. This is who we are and must no longer be viewed as failure.

In 1984, I enlisted in the United States Air Force and was stationed at Travis Air Force Base in Northern California. I spent three of my four years trying to get out. Please don't get me wrong. It was a great developmental experience and made me who I am today; however, as they say, "the military ain't no place for a Black man." Although I loved it, it hated me. Initially, when I arrived at Lackland Air Force Base for basic training, I was made dorm chief. As I would find out later, it was an honor bestowed on the biggest guy in the flight (your fifty-man cohort). I was off to a good start, or so I thought, until the neighboring drill sergeant would have his say, and I was demoted the mail boy. The Southern and Midwestern Airmen (as most were) customarily called New Yorkers slick as they did me, and you were treated with suspicion. I would be harassed from here on out, starting with a collection of my former resentful team leaders for not living up to their expectations. Upon arrival at the David Grant Medical Center at Travis AFB, my base of permanent duty, I was determined to get off to an amazing start. I polished my shoes, got my hair cut, and had all my blues dry-cleaned and ready to go. I drove an Audi 4000 at the time. I regularly cleaned it and parked it out in front of the clinic so I could periodically peek at its awesomeness through the window. My military occupational specialty (MOS) was behavioral science technician or mental health counselor. That first week in the outpatient clinic, I recall a meeting with my NCOIC, who was a tech sergeant at the time (after fifteen years of service). He asked, among other things, how I planned to spend my time in the service. I told him, "First, I want to complete my bachelor's degree at the base education office and then apply for Officer Training School and aspire to become a lieutenant in a couple of years!" not realizing that I just said I wanted to be his boss, which didn't go over very well. Talk about first impressions. He just looked at me with a blank stare and wished me luck as if to say, "Over my dead body, you will." When I look back on those times, I would have hated me too as I was a bit full of myself and seemed to lack all humility. I had no idea at the time how arrogant and judgmental that may have sounded, among other self-important outbursts, but over the next three years, I felt they did everything possible to have me dishonorably discharged. By the end, I was defeated and didn't even care; I just wanted to get out. I was convinced I was getting this treatment solely because I was an African American, and I was being persecuted. I felt entitled to behave this way and believed I was being persecuted because of a cultural and traditional worldview—that I was just different, and that made me even more defensive. But I never imagined it could also be because I was an arrogant jerk too. This is how we sometimes can be blinded by our own preconceived notions if we are not careful. It's important to develop an objective sense of self-awareness for just this type of circumstance. You never know when it's them, or it could be you.

The importance of patience

According to Dr. Charles Manz, the core secret to successful failure is patience. Products and businesses go through three phases: vision, patience, and execution. Additionally, he asserts that the patience stage is the toughest and most uncomfortable. You have to take measures like cutting out parts of your vision while reacting to what the market is telling you. You get into trouble if you assume that you are going to reach critical mass too quickly because its most likely that you won't. It is in these ways, for example, that many of us lose patience and cannot handle this stage. Anytime we set out to learn or accomplish something new and significant, we likely face the same three stages and especially the challenge of the need for patience. The implication is clear: if we want to ultimately succeed in a significant way, we need to accept and be patient with the learning and development that goes along with facing challenges. The road to achievement is a long one, and those without patience—who want to see results immediately—may not be willing to walk it. Think of the recent critiques of millennials for being unwilling to "pay their dues" in an entry-level job, jumping from position to position rather than growing and learning.

In 2012, a study was conducted to examine whether patience helps students get things done. In five surveys they completed over the course of a semester, patient people of all stripes reported exerting more effort toward their goals than other people did. Those with inter-personal patience in particular made more progress toward their goals and were more satisfied when they achieved them (particularly if those goals were difficult) compared with less patient people. According to the study, those that experienced greater satisfaction with achieving their goals were also more patient, and these patient achievers were more content with their lives as a whole as well. In the most basic sense, patience is the propensity of a person to wait calmly in the face of frustration, adversity, or suffering. Patience is enacted across a wide range of circumstances and time frames. It is enacted (or not!)

in mundane activities such as waiting in traffic as well as in more significant and long-term situations such as parenting or dealing with a serious illness. Although it often involves a temporal or waiting component, patience is also called forth in situations with no direct focus on time (e.g., dealing with a difficult person). The study examined patience and well-being in the context of goal pursuit and achievement. Traditionally, researchers examining goal striving have tied certain goal characteristics and content to both hedonic and eudaemonic well-being. For example, goal achievement increases positive affect and hedonic happiness. In a second study conducted that year, researchers elicited ten goals from participants and then tracked goal achievement and patience on those goals across time. They hypothesized that (a) patient people exert more effort in pursuit of their goals and (b) pursue them with more patience than less patient people.

Previous research has shown that goal progress across the course of the quarter predicts well-being measured at the end of the quarter and that satisfaction with goal progress directly affects well-being, the theory being that patience enacted on goals will increase goal progress/satisfaction, which will then increase well-being, oftentimes being the product of acceptance and resolution found in failure however temporary. This is because when we fail, we suffer the shame of hitting the bottom, which, albeit difficult to recover from, alleviates the fear aspect. It is at this point we realize we still have all our legs, hands, and feet, and generally, we are still alive, healthy, and ready to fight our way back. The relief of rock bottom is the options are now available to us on the realization that we no longer have anything to lose. If we are patient with ourselves, we can now see the temporal nature of failure as we go through a complete transformation hidden in the experience of what we call rock bottom. However, for some, a consequence of psychological rock bottom is that we cease to recognize opportunities. You get so caught up in defeat that you don't sense when another road might be opening up. We see our situation as a conclusion. In reality, that's not really where it ends. The act of falling to the ground comes with a strange and unintended side effect of liberation. With nothing more to lose, we have a foundation, and this foundation limits downsides. With patience, the only place to go from there is up.

Although originally from New York, I moved with my kids from Berkeley, California, back to New York for the support of my family in 1991. At that time, I was a stockbroker for America's second-largest broker dealer. My wife had just died, and the firm allowed me to transfer to any location that I wished. So I chose our office at the Tishman Building at 666 Fifth Avenue, which is now owned by Jared Kushner. In order to get acclimated from a marketing perspective, I became very active in local civic organizations, which included an organization called the One Hundred Black Men of New York, Inc.—a national philanthropic nonprofit organization made up of America's most prominent African Americans. I quickly worked my

way up the ranks to secretary of the board, where I met David Vaughn, a senior board member of the organization at the time and mentor to the new starters like me. At that time, Vaughn was a mayoral appointee to head up off-track betting (OTB) under New York's first black mayor and member of the One Hundred Black Men of New York, Inc., David Dinkins.

One evening, David was dropping me off after a weekly meeting in Harlem. We were racing downtown through the streets with the single red light flashing on the roof, as was customary on government-issue cars at the time. It made me feel like a dignitary. I was commiserating on how difficult it was keeping up with everything while being a single dad. Although I loved being a broker, it required trading during the day and marketing at nights, cold calling, black-tie functions, client dinners, etc. Rushing home to deal with kids was not conducive to that line of work. I became a bad broker and a bad dad and needed to make a change. His advice to me would change the entire course of my life at the time. Simply put, he advised me to always put my kids first. I had to give this quite a bit of thought as I didn't know what he meant. On reflection, whichever direction I took from that moment forward, it should be in their best interest first and to the exclusion of all other considerations. With that, I quit my broker career and started looking at my options I had no plan, no degree, and lots of bills. With much thought and discussion, I realized I needed a new start, so I settled on graduate school—law school, to be exact—because an MBA involved math. I was not the strongest candidate as I had not completed undergraduate school yet, but this was not going to stop me. I knew this transition would take quite a bit of time, but I was patient, open-minded, and had enough with struggling for this lifetime. Over the next two years, I would take the Kaplan LSAT prep course twice, apply to ten schools at the cost of five hundred dollars in fees, and finally get accepted by two.

I completed my undergrad degree just in time to complete my law school application and get accepted. I told myself at the outset that of the 199 accredited law schools in the United States that I would apply to everyone until I was accepted. I didn't care how long it took. I was getting into one of them, and I was going to change my life and my children's lives. I knew doing a 180 to turn my life around would be a major undertaking and would take a great deal of time, but I also knew if I would only grant myself the time and be patient that anything would be possible. And it was. With patience, I did the impossible that year.

Eyes on the prize

When correcting failure or shortcomings, it's important to remember to stay solution focused and not be mesmerized by the nature of your errors, or you will be destined to repeat it. In fact, your mind will always trend toward that which it is focused on. Sometimes referred to as the law of attraction, this spiritual principle suggests that like attracts like and that positive thinking can usher in a more positive reality. Lao Tzu, an ancient Chinese philosopher, once said, "Watch your thoughts, they become your words; watch your words, they become your actions; watch your actions, they become your habits; watch your habits, they become your character; watch your character, it becomes your destiny." According to Proverbs 23:7 of the New King James Version (NKJV), "For as a man thinketh, so is he."

The idea that we attract what we put out has clearly been around since ancient times, and many credit Buddha with first introducing this notion to the world. Like attracts like even if we're not conscious of it. We're always "attracting" positivity or negativity based on the energy we're putting out ourselves. "We are all like magnets, both reflecting and attracting what we hold in our thoughts," explains spiritual author Shannon Kaiser. Or as professional intuitive Tanya Carroll Richardson puts it, the law of attraction is like "putting in an order with Spirit. Then Spirit will look around to find the best match for your manifestation request." Another principle of the law of attraction is that nature abhors a vacuum. This principle suggests that empty space cannot truly exist and always needs to be filled by something. As such, it's important to make space for positive change in your life by clearing out negativity. Like decluttering your desk or bedroom, your mind needs to be decluttered too so you have room to attract new things that better serve you. Another is that the present is always perfect. Perfecting the present moment is the last aspect of the law of attraction. It tells us that there will always be things to be unhappy about if you look for them, but rather than dwelling on things that are going wrong, finding ways to make things better is fundamental to shifting your reality into one that attracts what you desire. That's not to say you can't acknowledge negativity or feel emotions related to it. That gets into spiritual bypassing or toxic positivity territory. Rather, it's about doing what you can at the moment to improve any negative situation and letting the rest go.

However, positive thinking and belief alone won't make your dreams come true. You need to put in the work too! This means living in alignment with your goals and taking the necessary steps to bring them to life. Anyone prone to worry should also know that the law of attraction isn't a punishment. As Kaiser notes, "when people first learn and start to practice this law, sometimes they get worried that if they have bad thoughts or low vibrations, they can somehow mess up their life." Nobody is perfect, and we can use the law as "a mirror of our own mindset and self-worth" when we're working through a challenging phase. And always remember that at a certain point in manifestation, "it's important to surrender and let the Universe take the wheel," Richardson adds. "Opportunities, people, and resources can show up out of the blue, so be open to them." Things may not play out how you imagined (in fact, they probably won't), and that's okay. Very few people are fully aware of how much of an impact the law of attraction has on their day-to-day life. Unfortunately, so many of us are still blind to the potential that is locked deep within us. Consequently, it is all too easy to leave your thoughts and emotions unchecked. This sends out the wrong thoughts and attracts more unwanted emotions and events into your life.

Renowned motivational speaker Tony Robbins has a slightly different take on the law of attraction, whereby "energy flows where attention goes." According to Robbins, in order to get what you really want in life, you need a clear goal that has purpose and meaning behind it. Once this is in place, you can focus your energy on the goal and become obsessive about it. When you learn how to focus your energy, amazing things happen. You get insights that weren't available to you before. You run into people who seem magically put in your path to help you. You overhear conversations or stumble upon resources that further your plan. That's the secret of how energy flows where attention goes.

However, what happens when you're always picking out flaws or paying attention to the negative aspects of life? When you ascribe to Tony's belief that where focus goes, energy flows and are already committing to staying in a dark headspace, it means you will get more negativity because it's what you're concentrating on. In fact, it was the renowned Swiss psychiatrist Carl Jung (1875–1961), who taught us that whatever you resist persists. What he meant by that is the more you resist anything in life the more you bring it to you. The reason you attract whatever you resist is because you are powerfully focused on it with strong feelings and emotion, and what you focus on with any emotion, you bring to you. This is why anti-war rallies often break out in violence. It's also why a protest against injustice leads to innocent people getting arrested. And it's why a politician that most people despise seems to get reelected every single time. By focusing with strong feelings on what you don't want, you can't help but attract it.

The American rapper Biggie Smalls' debut album *Ready to Die* came out in 1994, and he was killed a few short years later in a senseless act of gun violence. Tupac Shakur regularly sang about death with songs like "I Wonder if Heaven Got a Ghetto," "If I Die 2nite," and "Death around the Corner." He, too, was killed in a senseless act of gun violence not long after. The list of rappers that succumb to violent and untimely deaths is too long to list here; however, you would be hard-pressed to make an argument against the fact that violent lifestyles, lyrics, and subject matter didn't play a significant role. In fact, I have seen this phenomenon play out in my own life. While on active duty, I married my high school sweetheart, who I knew since I was in ninth grade. Her parents never liked me or me hanging around anyway. In order to visit, I regularly had to see her behind their backs. Ultimately, they knew I was in the picture and became a regular presence in their dysfunctional lives. The dad was a functional alcoholic, and the mom was extremely abusive—but never in front of me.

While in high school, I spent a good deal of time over at her house, and they became very comfortable with me. Their fights continued in my presence and often got way out of hand: cursing, breaking furniture, and physical altercations. While in the midst of the fighting, she would regularly make threats that she would kill herself, and on occasion, I would intervene in her attempts to cut herself or even drink various poisons. How much of this was for show and theatrics, I will never know, but it was pretty disturbing nonetheless. I often told her when things calmed down to never make such threats as they will come true. Like Robbins said, by focusing strong feelings on what you don't want, you can't help but attract it. Some years later, I thought she would benefit by getting out of this environment, and we got married and moved to northern California. However, the erratic emotionalism, violent outbursts, and manipulative threats of suicide never stopped, and we didn't last either. Shortly after our last breakup, she ultimately committed suicide. To what degree the fixation on death, violence, and dying played a role in these instances, we may never quantify, but I feel strongly that nothing good can come from taunting death.

Keeping your eyes on the prize requires that you develop an abundance mindset. Choosing gratitude and appreciation over criticism and negativity leads to attracting more of the things you can appreciate and be grateful for. When you look in the mirror, do you see your beautiful smile, or do you instantly notice how old you're starting to look? If you focus on the positives, you'll radiate confidence and be attractive to others. The next time you're in a new situation or environment, practice the "Where focus goes, energy flows" way of thinking. If you're outdoors, notice the cool breeze or the smell of nearby flowers. If you're inside, try to spot interesting decor or architectural styles. If you meet new people in this situation, ask thoughtful questions and listen deeply to the answers. Focus on at least one personality trait you admire in each person you talk to. How do you feel when you leave this new situation? How does this differ from similar situations you've been in when you've spent all your time thinking about how you'd rather be somewhere else? When you focus on the positives, you'll be amazed at how much easier it becomes to unlock an extraordinary life.

"Where focus goes, energy flows" is not just a concept that helps in appreciating life; it's a powerful tool in achieving your goals and making the best out of failure. When you have a clear vision of your goal and devote your energy and focus to it, ordinary time suckers like social media, saying yes to things you really want to say no to, and losing track of time effortlessly fall away. All of us have downtime—the time between work, errands, family time, etc.—that we can take advantage of. The difference between those who are obsessive about a goal and devote focus and energy to it and everyone else is that most people are stuck in reaction mode. Instead of developing a clear plan, the majority of people simply deal with situations and issues as they arise and never really get ahead. Their focus is so dispersed that energy can never flow directly toward achieving their big goal. While they may still reach small goals or accomplish tasks, they'll never get what they really want. Having a clear result or outcome and learning how to focus your energy on it immediately changes your behavior, giving you the momentum you need to take small actions daily that will lead to geometric results. This momentum enables you to dig out and make the necessary corrections that allow you to stay the course.

Big success equals big failure—fail big and fail often

Famous Actor Will Smith said about failure that "we should fail early, fail often, and fail forward." He is always a little bit frustrated when people have a negative relationship with failure. According to Smith, "failure is a massive part of being able to be successful. You have to get comfortable with failure," adding that "what people don't seem to understand is that you have to actually seek failure. Failure is what you seek when you go to the gym. You work out and are actually seeking to take your muscles to the point where you get to failure because that's where the adaptation is, where the growth is." Successful people extract the lessons from failure, and they use that energy and the wisdom to come around to the next phase of success. Smith adds, "You have got a take a shot and live at the edge of your capabilities. You have got to live where you are almost certain you're going to fail. That's the reason for practice. Practice is controlled failure. You're getting to your limit until your body gets to the point that all of a sudden, your body makes the adjustment, and then you can do it. Failure actually helps you to recognize the areas where you need to evolve. So fail early, fail often, and fail forward."

Not only do we win through failure, but we may also suffer in some circumstances by avoiding failure, such as in the investment banking industry, which is organized around seeking out failure and managing in that failure in the form of assuming and managing risks. According to the US Securities and Exchange Commission's investor.gov website, *risk* is defined as the "degree of uncertainty and/or potential financial loss inherent in an investment decision." Understand that all investments involve some degree of risk, even those appearing safe; playing it safe, avoiding risk and failure, may cost you. In this world, investing in just one asset class (buying shares in an individual company or only buying investment properties) is risky (i.e., placing all your eggs in one basket). In fact, among the principles of the modern portfolio theory is the idea of investment diversification. Modern portfolio theory (MPT) is a collection of theories on how risk-averse investors can construct portfolios to maximize expected return based on a given level of market risk. As a practical matter, risk aversion implies that most people should invest in multiple asset classes or diversify their assets across different types of assets. Basically, to investment banking professionals, seeking out failure in the form of risk is essential in capital markets investing and necessary to make great gains. This is a discourse where the bigger the risk of loss the greater the potential for rewards, otherwise known as the "risk-reward relationship." The issue is that risk must be managed to tilt the metric to the investor's advantage. Every trade has a seller and a buyer, making your state of mind of paramount importance. If you are in a risk-averse mental framework and afraid to fail on the trade, then you are likely to interpret a further fall in stocks as additional confirmation of your sell bias. If instead your framework is positive, you will interpret the same event as a buying opportunity. Capital markets investing is a discourse where your fear of failure actually may hurt your profitability. The challenge of investing is compounded by the fact that our brains, which excel at resolving ambiguity in the face of a threat, are less well equipped to navigate the long-term intelligently. Since none of us can predict the future, successful investing requires planning and discipline. Unfortunately, when reason is in apparent conflict with our instincts—about markets or a hot stock, for example—it is our instincts that typically prevail. Our reptilian brain wins out over our rational brain, as it so often does in other facets of our lives. And as we have seen, investors trade too frequently and often at the wrong time.

One way our brains resolve conflicting information is to seek out safety in numbers. In the animal kingdom, this is called moving with the herd, and it serves a very important purpose: helping ensure survival. Even the so-called smart money falls prey to a herd mentality: one study aptly titled "Thy Neighbor's Portfolio" found that professional mutual fund managers were more likely to buy or sell a particular stock if other managers in the same city were also buying or selling. This comfort is costly. The surge in buying activity and the resulting bullish sentiment is self-reinforcing, propelling markets to react even faster. That leads to overvaluation and the inevitable crash when sentiment reverses. Even though the role of instinct and human emotions in driving speculative bubbles has been well documented in popular books, newspapers, and magazines for hundreds of years, these factors were virtually ignored in conventional financial and economic models until the 1970s.

This is especially surprising given that in 1951, Harry Markowitz published two very important papers on this phenomenon. The first, entitled "Portfolio Selection," published in the *Journal of Finance*, led to the creation of MPT together with the widespread adoption of its important ideas such as asset allocation and diversification, mentioned above. It earned Harry Markowitz a Nobel Prize in Economics. The second paper, entitled "The Utility of Wealth" and published in the prestigious *Journal of Political Economy*, was about the propensity of people to hold insurance (safety) and to buy lottery tickets at the same time. It delved deeper into the psychological aspects of investing but was largely forgotten for decades.

The field of behavioral finance really came into its own through the pioneering work of two academic psychologists, Amos Tversky and Daniel Kahneman, who challenged conventional wisdom about how people make decisions involving risk. Their work garnered Kahneman the Nobel Prize in Economics in 2002. Behavioral finance and neuroeconomics are relatively new fields of study that seek to identify and understand human behavior and decision-making with regard to choices involving trade-offs between risk and reward. Of particular interest are the human biases that prevent individuals from making fully rational financial decisions in the face of uncertainty. As behavioral economists have documented, our propensity for herd behavior is just the tip of the iceberg. Kahneman and Tversky, for example, showed that people who were asked to choose between a certain loss and a gamble in which they could either lose more money or break even would tend to choose the double down (that is, gamble to avoid the prospect of losses), a behavior the authors called loss aversion or alternatively, failure aversion. Building on this work, Hersh Shefrin and Meir Statman, professors at the University of Santa Clara Leavey School of Business, have linked the propensity for loss aversion to investors' tendency to hold losing investments too long and to sell winners too soon. They called this bias the disposition effect.

Behavioral finance treats biases as mistakes that, in academic parlance, prevent investors from thinking rationally and cause them to hold "suboptimal" portfolios. Effective decision-making requires us to balance our reptilian brain, which governs instinctive thinking, with our rational brain, which is responsible for strategic thinking. Instinct must integrate with experience. Put another way, behavioral biases are nothing more than a series of complex trade-offs between risk and reward. When the stock market is taking off, for example, a failure to rebalance by selling winners is considered a mistake. The same goes for a failure to add to a position in a plummeting market. In essence, learning from the mistakes and improving your returns by correcting your position in the market and your strategy—this is foundational for managing risk. What, then, does all this mean when it comes to failure? In the words of Wayne Gretzky—the greatest hockey player of all time—"You miss 100 percent of the shots you don't take." We must not run from risk but learn to manage risk in order to reap the reward as a riskless portfolio could also be described as a return-less portfolio. This can also be said of fearing failure in general. We must get comfortable with the possibility and eventuality of failing at any new undertaking in order to get through the unknown challenges blocking access to the successes that may lie on the other side. Most people don't reach their dream not because of failure; most people don't live their dream because they give up. You see, it's not the failure that stops us but that most stop at their first failure! Those who succeed don't stop at one failure. They don't stop at ten failures. They don't stop at one hundred, one thousand, or millions of failures. They say, "This is my goal, and I will do whatever it takes to achieve it. I will learn the lessons from any failures. I will learn fast, I will work hard, I will work smarter, and I will not quit until my dream is a reality!"

Failure makes winners stronger; failure makes winners hungrier. But it also makes most give up. It makes most feel worthless. Winners don't enjoy failure, but they would never let failure stop them. Next time you encounter failure, you must remember that every great thing on this planet is here because the creator learned not only what did work but more from what did not work. When we were kids, we didn't stop at failure. When we first learned to ride a bike, it was failure after failure, and when we got knocked down, time after time, we got up and pushed forward until we achieved our goal of riding the bike. We didn't make excuses; we just told ourselves to get back on the bike, learned why we failed, and made sure we didn't fall again. This is what made us strong. Failure is not the end of the story; it is the start of your comeback story. If failure was the end of your story, there would be no greats like Jordan, Einstein, Edison, or Oprah Winfrey. If these people stopped at failure, the world would not be filled with their greatness as it is today. Failure is nothing but a lesson to the winner. Failure is nothing but motivation to the winner. Failure is fuel. No one likes to fail, but the difference between those that win and those that lose in life is the winner decides a better meaning for *failure*. The only way you can call it a failure is if you quit.

Les Brown, famous failure and motivational speaker, tells a story of when he was in in fifth grade and was identified as an EMR, "educable mentally retarded," and kept back from the fifth grade. He recounts that he failed again when he was in the eighth grade.

He said he has no college training to this day. However, one man changed his life, and he will never forget him. And his name was Mr. Washington. At the telling of this story, Mr. Washington was in his 80s, and although he was blind from glaucoma, he gave Les a different vision of himself. Les recalled waiting on another student in his classroom when Mr. Washington came in and said, "Young man, go to the board and work this problem out for me." Les replied, "I can't do that," and Mr. Washington said, "Why not?" to which Les replied, "I am an EMR, sir. I'm in special education." And the students started laughing. They said that Leslie was the dumb twin as the students continued to laugh at him, at which point, Mr. Washington came from behind his desk, looked at Les, and said, "Don't you ever say that again. Someone's opinion of you does not have to become your reality." Les also famously recounts another story where he fell on some hard times early in his career and had to sleep in his office. At one point, the security guard met him in the lobby of the building and said, "Excuse me, Mr. Brown, can we see you for a moment?" And he said yes and walked up to the desk. And he gave him an envelope and said, "Would you mind reading it here?" The note was from the management and said, "This is an office tower. It's not a hotel. Please do not sleep in your office." Les told security that he just worked long hours in creating his business, that he was an entrepreneur, and that right now, things were bad; but they're not going to be this way always. He went on to ask for the opportunity to continue to operate in this manner. He told them he was not trying to make this his home. He told of how hard it was, coming through the lobby and sometimes hearing them laugh at "the guy talking about becoming successful, and look at him. He's bathing in the bathroom upstairs on the twenty-first floor. He sleeps on the floor, him and two other dreamers." Les Brown's message to those of us that have experienced some hardships and failings is "Don't give up on your dreams!" He stated that no one could have convinced him that by holding on, by continuing to push forward, and by continuing to run toward his dream that one day, he would have his own talk show.

All wins are not winning, and all losses are not losing

Quoting novelist Ian McEwan, "selfishness is written in our hearts. The fact is compassion is in our hearts too." The challenge when you're heading for the finish line is knowing when to let compassion take the lead. Each of us encounters this kind of choice every day, and it can be an opportunity to lend a hand when someone needs our help at work or to stop what we're doing listen when a friend needs someone to talk to. Making the right choice when it temporarily distracts from our progress is the challenge. Sometimes we need to stay on task, but sometimes it's even more important to help someone else—a wise lesson is in learning that the shortest route to victory may be a trap that can cause us to lose more than we gain.

Illustrating the foregoing, consider Valerie Kondos Field ("Coach K"), the retired head coach of the UCLA Women's Gymnastics team, a position that she held for 29 years. In a recent TED Talk, Coach K provides two examples on what's wrong with today's "win at all cost culture", in sports and in life; and why it sometimes may even culminate in a loss where it counts most-by—in that may produce broken human beings. She opens with a question, "…is all winning success"? This coming from a coach that knows winning, as she led UCLA gymnastics to seven national championships, was inducted into the UCLA athletic Hall of Fame and even voted the coach of the century by the PAC 12 conference.

In all of her achievements, Coach "K" understands that winning does not always equal success, very well. She shared how in America, this attitude, is a crisis that has permeated our schools, our businesses, as well as our politics. She observes that, winning at all costs has become acceptable. Stating that,

> "...as a society we honor the people at the top of the pyramid. We effusively applaud those people who win championships, win elections, and awards but sadly quite often those same people are leaving their institutions as damaged human being; sadly, with straight A's, kids are leaving school damaged; with awards and medals. Athletes often leave teams damaged, both, emotionally and mentally, not just physically. And with huge profits, employees often leave their companies damaged. We have become so hyper focused on that end result, and when the end result is a win, the human component of how we got there often gets swept under the proverbial rug and so does the damage. ...We need to redefine success. Win or lose, real success is developing champions in life, not for your team, not for your business, ...not even for your Christmas card bragging rights, sorry."

To add context to these observations, Coach K shares a couple of stories about what she learned about her own hubris and maintaining this toxic win-at-all-cost mentality. She tells of how she started out as a coach, knowing nothing about how to develop a "team culture", other than to mimic the old school success stories. This culminated in becoming, in her own words, a "tough talking, tough minded, relentless, unsympathetic, bullish, and oftentimes down right mean" coach, whose only thought was to figure out how to win. It was no wonder that her first few seasons as a head coach were abysmal failures, so much so, that after putting up with her brash coaching style for a few years, the team held a meeting to provide two hours, of example after example, of how her attitude and approach towards the team was hurtful and demeaning. The team explained how, they wanted to be "supported, not belittled". They want to be "coached up, not torn down". They want to be "motivated, not pressured or bullied". This was truly a watershed moment for Coach K, as it was at this moment that she chose to change. She realized that being a dogmatic dictator may produce compliant good little soldiers, but it doesn't develop champions in life. It's much easier, in any walk of life, to dictate and give orders, than to actually figure out how to moti-vate someone to want to be better. She needed to fortify her student athletes as whole human beings not just athletes who won. On this realization, her definition of success shifted, from only focusing on winning, to developing a coaching philosophy. A philosophy that develops champions in life through sport. Coach K understood, that if she did this well enough, that champion mentality would translate to the competition floor—and she would ultimately discover that it did.

According to Coach K, the key ingredient was to develop trust through patience, respectful honesty, and accountability. In other words, to develop a culture of "tough love"; the application of which, would soon be tested on Katelyn Ohashi and Kyla Ross. It is in these two accounts, that she shares her most significant lesson on the power of humility and how sometime when we lose, we win. In each case, in order to tease out the highest performance, personal challenges of the student athletes had to be addressed. However, to address those challenges Coach K had to build trust and develop respect, as well as to create a safe space where they could share and be regarded in the entirety of their being and not just be hustled for their talents. Only then would she see the peak performance of these two, star athletes. With Katelyn, Coach K found her broken, in body, mind and spirit. She came up in the sport, like so many others, damaged and rebellious, to the point where she was no longer able to do gymnastics at the level at which she was recruited. She recalls that Katelyn was burned out and simply no longer interested in ever being great again. In response, Coach K would embark on the painfully slow process of building trust and instilling within her that she was truly cared for as a whole human being. It wasn't just about winning but about the whole person behind the performance. Highlighting this part of this strategy would mean, Coach K decided to only talk to Katelyn about gymnastics while in the gym. While, on the street, however, they would talk about everything else, school, boys, families, friends, and hobbies. Coach K recalled, that she, encouraged Katelyn to find things outside of her sport that brought her joy and through that process allowed Katelyn to rediscover her self-love and self-worth and slowly bring the joy back to her gymnastics. With a new found determination Katelyn went on to earn the NCAA title on the floor and she helped UCLA win a 7th NCAA championship in 2018. What Coach K found through this experience, according to this talk, demonstrates that, "one of the greatest gifts we can give another human being, is to silence our minds from the need to be right or the need to formulate the appropriate response and truly listen when someone else is talking. …in silencing our minds, we actually hear our own fears, and inadequacy which can help us formulate our response with more clarity and empathy."

A similar approach was taken with another member of the team, Kyla Ross, who was believed to be one of the greatest gymnasts in the history of the sport. She's a national champion, a world champion, and an Olympic champion; and unfortunately, among the many victims of Larry Nassar the former USA Gymnastics team Doctor, who was later convicted of being a serial child molester. Not one for small talk, until now, she had not revealed her abuse to anyone except Coach K. Coach K felt it was extremely important at that time to provide a safe space for Kayla and her teammates to bring these issues out into the open and orchestrated this through a series of team meetings. Later that year UCLA won the national championship. It would later be revealed that the reason performance improved among the team was largely due to the fact that they had addressed the elephant in the room, the abuse raking the sport at the time and the tragedy that rocked the world. Kayla said, to Coach K, that she literally felt herself walk taller as the season went on, and when she walked out onto that championship floor, she said she felt invincible. Simply because she had been heard. About these experiences, Coach K surmised that,

> "...As parents, as coaches, as leaders, we can no longer lead from a place where winning is our only metric of success and where our ego sits center stage. Because it has been proven, that that process produces broken human beings. ...it is absolutely possible to produce and train champions in life, in every single walk of life, without compromising the human spirit. Spirit, it starts with defining success for yourself and those under your care and then consistently self-examining whether your actions are in alignment with your goals. We are all coaches in some capacity we all have a collective responsibility to develop champions in life for our world. That is what real success looks like and in the world of athletics that is what we call a win-win!"

Taking the concept even one step further, consider the story that gave us the Pyrrhic Victory. Col. J. T. Bell (1942) of the US Army, writing of his experience with Hitler, analogizes him to the king of Epirus. Bell recalls that twenty-two centuries ago, a despotic warrior king gave his name to the type of victory or success that is gained at so great a cost that few benefits are obtained by the victory. In those days, the nations of the Balkans aspired to rule the then known (to them) world of Pyrrhus, led by the aggressors of that period in the first battle between the Greeks and the Romans at Heracles. Victory on the battlefield was followed by other victories and pursuits while they occupied many conquered cities. The king of Epirus was a skillful tactician and a brilliant leader on the battlefield. But he ruled in a despotic way, and the conquered cities rose against him whenever there was hope of a successful resistance. The king's victories on the battlefield were simply military successes; he established nothing of permanence. He did nothing to better the conditions of his own people or the people of the lands he occupied. He was merely a despot governing to suit his own whims and fancies. His victories were, as they came to be called, Pyrrhic victories. The term has remained as part of the languages and will probably remain as such long after Pyrrhus's present-day counterpart has passed into history (referring to Hitler). Winning sometimes delivers you setbacks and failures while losing is not always a loss. Sometimes your losing can be a gift to a child or a friend that allows them to experience joy and confidence because of their victory. And sometimes when you lose at first but persevere and try your best to turn things around, your ultimate victory can be all the greater. That's why sometimes when you lose, you win.

Dorothee Loorbach used to be exceptionally successful in her job, earning a lot of money over the course of her career in marketing. She tells the story of how she unmasked her relation to money and reveals her personal life-changing learnings from her six-month project of becoming financially carefree. Loorbach had left her well-paid job to become an entrepreneur, and very soon, she could buy anything she wanted, which, according to Loorbach, was a lot. Her impulse purchases included a brand-new car and a house as her entire life was all about fun. She had some amazing memories; however, she just wanted more—to do something that would last, something that mattered. Around that time, she started working with students, and for the first time in her life, people would come up to her and say, "Thank you. You've changed my life." This was so valuable that she would do it if even for just a little bit of money. She even considered doing it for free—or at least until she reached a financial setback that could ruin her as an entrepreneur. Of course, that's exactly what happened in the summer of 2016 while all schools were closed. She had no income for over two months or so and received five envelopes at the same time from the tax services demanding that she pay for her glory days immediately.

This cost her all her savings, leaving her with only a few coins that she found between the cushions of the sofa, in her coat pocket, and in the car; three euros; and 97¢ in the bank. Then the realization hit that in only two days, her daughter would come back from staying with her father—on her birthday, and she couldn't afford to bake her a cake. She was devastated at the realization that she only had only forty-eight hours to prove to herself that she was a good mother. She then did the most terrifying and the most embarrassing thing she has ever done in her life: expose herself publicly as a failure. To Loorbach, the best place to start to put your life back together again was at rock bottom. She gave away the last of her money, and with absolutely nothing left, the only way was up. She called her plan the money project and published a video on Facebook, stating that she had failed gloriously as an entrepreneur and that she was totally broke and was determined to change her situation to learn anything she could about entrepreneurship, business, and money to enhance her financial intelligence. At this point, she was determined to become free of financial stress within six months. She would write a book about it, and this book sold right away for $10 a copy. The first day, she sold sixty-four books and has never felt richer in her entire life. This meant she could now buy a big a birthday cake and have a proper birthday for her daughter. All this time, she had been thinking that the money project was about money and business, but deep down, it was about something completely different: value and life.

She identified the ten lessons she learned through her foray with financial failure and ruin. However, for our purposes, we shall highlight only a few of these lessons: First, she observed that money is important even though she learned otherwise, and as a result, she had never managed it appropriately. Money doesn't make you a bad person, just more of the person you already are. The second lesson was that money equals time. As soon as we start our working years, we start exchanging time for money, which she describes as a problem. She observes that we can always make more money, but we can never make more time. She started to exchange her time for far too little money, as she could barely survive. She decided that she would spend her time more consciously from now on. The third lesson is that money equals value. She has always seen herself as a confident person, but she didn't value herself accordingly. She came to realize that the way you treat yourself is a reflection of the way you see yourself, and she recounts that she has been treating herself like crap and a terrible example to set for her daughter. She learned to see herself as a person of value, and this remains an ongoing practice. The fourth lesson is that what people say doesn't matter. "You're a fraud" and "How can you do this to your child?" were just a few of the comments that she received. The hateful ones were on her time line on Facebook, but the quiet ones, hid safely in her inbox, confessed only to her that they had screwed up too. She was also thankful for her haters whether they were the strangers on her social media time line or even some of her own friends talking badly about her behind her back because they taught her that nothing is ever personal, not really. What people say about you and what people think about you, comes from their view of the world—it's from their opinions, their values, and their experiences. Maybe they're having a bad day, or they're very insecure and unhappy. It has nothing to do with you. In fact, Don Miguel Ruiz echoed this sentiment in his book *The Four Agreements*, stating that "whatever happens around you, don't take it personally… Nothing other people do is because of you. It is because of themselves." The fifth lesson is that what people say matters most when "people" is you! Because the person with the most opinions about you and the person who talks to you the most is you, and you tend to believe yourself! So be kind! The sixth lesson is really simple. Everything Loorbach learned, she could have learned from her grandmother because the essence is "Spend less and invest more wisely." Lesson seven is that "simple is not always easy." According to Parkinson's law, your expenses will always rise to match your income. This is why most people retire poor and why lottery winners tend to end up with less money a few years after they won than what they had before.

When I moved to the East Coast, shortly after the death of my wife, I thought that these events would spell the death of my career as well and that this would be the end of my very short run at turning the tables against my own failures. It was only couple of years prior that I had great success at a regional broker dealer and parlayed that into the opportunity I had at Smith Barney, the second-largest broker dealer in America behind Merrill Lynch at the time. I made it work because of hard work and lots of cold calling followed by home visits. In those days, it was the closest thing to a door-to-door salesman as you could get without being a door-to-door salesman. Basically, the asset-raising component of the job required time and lots of it. I could not imagine how I could keep up the activities required of the job while being a single dad, of not one, but two children under five years old, and in NYC of all places.

I came back to New York for the help of mother, but unbeknownst to me, she had issues all on her own much worse than mine. Mom was good for taking on more than she could handle and had recently became foster parent to four siblings from the city—all under the age of ten. She only wanted two of them but, not wanting to split up the family, took in all of them. However, she failed to tell me about this when she volunteered to assist with my two kids. Also, at her house were my younger brother (fifteen years old), my uncle (who seemed to be a constant presence), and her soon-to-be husband (the entertainer with a gambling problem), all of which depended on her for support in some way or another. Suffice it to say, I already agreed to stay with my dad, who lived in Queens nearby. The kids stayed with my mother, and I would pick them up on the weekends. This arrangement didn't work for very long as there was just too much going on over there, so I moved the kids in with me. I hobbled along for a while longer, trying to make it work, but ultimately would quit and change careers altogether. I became a father at nineteen years old, and for so long, I used to think that having kids at an early age meant the end of my life and ambition. But I could not have been more wrong. In fact, raising those children gave me the life and opportunities that I would ultimately have and provided me the personal development I needed to thrive.

We often complain about circumstances and conditions that we find ourselves in and feel, "This is not what I wanted"! However, since when did we know what we wanted, what was even available as an option for our lives, or what was best for us at any given point in time? The truth of the matter is that we don't know and never did. We just have to act for the sake of principle, move forward in purpose, and trust that the process will lead us to the best possible outcome in every circumstance—this is intuition or spirit. I was such a mix of emotions, and none of them good—angry, depressed, sad, and ashamed—because I believed so much in what I had and subsequently lost. I thought I came so far with so little that I could never replicate my past success however overrated it was in hindsight. I never thought that the present opportunities could have forestalled or blocked what I was to become had I not gotten past it. Sometimes what failure does is create options and expose us to the future that we could never have imagined had we continued succeeding in a lesser direction. By putting my children first, I stepped out on faith, giving up the job, and I changed careers entirely. Because of my children, I worked as hard as I did, made the sacrifices that I made, and met the people I met in my life; and it was because of them that I eventually got it right. It was because of them that I was motivated to study in law school and write papers at two in the morning. In hindsight, what I became, like Marcus Aurelius said, was because of them. The obstacle in the way became the way.

Practice does not make perfect; it's sustained effort that matters most

Fear of failure is one of the biggest obstacles to living a full and rewarding life. Avoiding mistakes or doing a poor job in performing a new activity can cause us to not even try. Even the best in the world in any given endeavor made many, many mistakes on their way to becoming the best. Most of the finest musicians in the world hit many sour notes in their hours and hours of practice. Babe Ruth, the baseball player, did hit more home runs than anyone else in his generation, but his strikeouts far outnumbered his homers. The Olympic Games are one of the greatest symbols of excellence. The best athletes from around the world gather every four years to compete. Much attention and acclaim are bestowed on those who proved to be the best in competition, and they walk away with the gold medal in this sport. However, in our admiration of these champions, we sometimes lose sight of the real purpose and meaning of the Olympics.

An *Irish Times* article dated November 21, 2000, discussed a recent controversy on the Paralympics, as there appeared to be "some confusion regarding the notion that learning, work, sports, creativity, productivity are best served by focusing and valuing the effort involved in these pursuits. There is no suggestion that the inevitable different levels of achievements attained should not be celebrated. But excellence is much more likely to emerge when people's attention is on the effort and process of learning. In any case, excellence cannot be achieved without considerable effort; indeed, when excellence is not attained, the problem generally will be in the level of effort shown."

Effort is when we do battle in the dojo of ourselves, and through regular practice, this sustained effort leeches into our performance, making us great. People who tend to be focused on results or success divide their energies between the process and end result, which also means that their minds are operating both in the present and in the future. As a consequence, performance anxiety is the most common kind of fear and can be chronic and even crippling for some individuals. Failure and success are integral to learning; for the mature person, both provide ongoing challenges. However, some people live for success and have a consequent dread of failure, and such fixations limit rather than enhance their creativity and productivity.

Bill Gates puts it well when he said, "Success is the greatest impediment to progress." It is unfortunate that success and failure are used as motivating forces: the result is either to extinguish or diminish a love of learning or to create perfectionism or addiction to success. People who love learning and work are driven by excitement and challenge; those who attempt to prove themselves through achievements whether academic or nonacademic are driven by fear. The best form of competition is self-competition, where individuals are encouraged and supported to challenge themselves instead of looking over their shoulder at what others are doing. So many people, young and old, do not take on new challenges for fear of being not good enough and being compared to others. The wisdom of their avoidance is often missed by a society that is success and competition driven.

It is difficult to overstate the value of practice. In his 2004 article entitled "Reframing the Mind", Daniel T. Willingham summarizes why practice is so important and reviews the different effects of intense short-term practice versus sustained, long-term practice. For a new skill to become automatic or for new knowledge to become long-lasting, sustained practice, beyond the point of mastery, is necessary. Intuition tells us that more practice leads to better memory. Research tells us something more precise: memory in either the short- or long-term requires ongoing practice. Studying material that one already knows is called overlearning. Because memory is prone to forgetting, we cannot learn material to a criterion and then expect the memory to stay at that level for very long. Anticipating the effect of forgetting dictates that we continue our practice beyond the mastery we desire. Working memory is, to put it colloquially, the place in the mind where thought happens. It is often called the bottleneck of the mind because there is a limited amount of space in working memory. That is why it is difficult to mentally divide 34,516 by 87. It is hard to simultaneously maintain the numbers, employ the processes for long division, and update the answer as you derive it. According to Willingham, this space limitation is relevant not just to mental arithmetic but to most types of problems he would like his students to solve such as writing a clear laboratory report, reading an essay with deep understanding, or seeing the links between historical events.

Our ability to think would be limited if there were not ways to overcome the space constraint of working memory. One of the more important mechanisms is the development of automaticity. When cognitive processes (e.g., reading, writing grammatically, reading a map, identifying the dependent variable in a science experiment, using simple mathematical procedures) become automatic, they demand very little space in working memory. They occur rapidly, and they often occur without conscious effort.

For example, as you are reading this book, the process of reading is very likely automatic for you. You do not need to laboriously piece together the letters of each word to puzzle out its meaning. Your mind seems to divine the meaning of prose immediately and without effort on your part. Most of the time, automaticity is helpful rather than disruptive. Picture a beginning reader slowly puzzling out the word *blue*. Doing so consumes all of working memory, so it is difficult for the student to follow the plot of the story in which the word appears. Once reading is automatic, however, precious working memory resources can be devoted to considering the meaning of a text, the effectiveness of its argument, and so on. Automaticity is important not only in reading but in all mental life. Consider how difficult it would be to navigate an unfamiliar city by car if you had to focus on how hard to press the accelerator and brake, how far to turn the steering wheel, when to monitor your mirrors, and all of the other components of driving that have become automatized. Automaticity is vital in education because it allows us to become more skillful in mental tasks. An effective writer knows the rules of grammar and usage to the point of automaticity and knows automatically to begin a paragraph with a topic sentence, include relevant details, etc. The effective mathematician invokes important math facts and procedures automatically. Readers who are able to visualize a map of the world will find various books and assignments easier to read (and learn more from them). In each field, certain procedures are used again and again. Those procedures must be learned to the point of automaticity so that they no longer consume working memory space. Only then will the student be able to bypass the bottleneck imposed by working memory and move on to higher levels of competence.

The issue here is that development of automaticity for generalized skills depends on high levels of practice (e.g., Shiffrin and Schneider, 1984). There is no substitute. Ensuring consistent, sustained practice is the most reliable way to ensure that a student will become an effective reader, writer, or scientist. Following a complex written argument, writing a convincing essay, or engaging in scientific reasoning are all skills that are enabled by the automatization of each discipline's basics. When asked how an expert gained such a high level of skill, nonexperts usually attribute the success to innate talent. Experts themselves, however, tell a different story. They attribute their success to practice and to the ability to maintain concentration during long practice sessions (Ericsson, 1996). (The importance of practice doesn't mean that innate talent is meaningless, of course; practice is necessary for excellence but may not be sufficient to ensure it.) Research studies indicate that experts are right, at least in that they do practice a great deal. Descriptive studies (Roe, 1953) of eminent scientists indicate that the most important factor predicting their success is not innate talent or intelligence but the willingness to work hard for extended periods of time. This commitment to practice was reinforced by a large-scale study (Bloom, 1985) in which experts in athletics, science, and the arts were interviewed along with their parents and teachers. Bloom proposed that the training of an expert typically involved four stages. The future expert was usually introduced to the domain under playful conditions as a child.

His or her promise was noted, and in the second stage, lessons were provided usually with a teacher or coach who worked well with children. And regular practice habits were established. In the third stage, an internationally recognized teacher or coach was engaged, usually requiring a significant commitment of resources from the parents as well as dedicated and likely exclusive study by the child. In the fourth stage, the student had absorbed all that he or she could from teachers and began to develop his or her personal contribution to the field.

Recent research that measures practice time more carefully paints a similar picture. Two conclusions may be drawn from this research: that experts engage in a great deal of practice and that even among very able performers, the best are those who have practiced more. Evidenced by the "ten-year rule," which proposes that a great deal of practice, and not just talent, is a prerequisite for expertise. Called the ten-year rule because individuals must practice intensively for at least ten years before they are ready to make a substantive contribution to their field. What about prodigies like Mozart, who began composing at the age of six? Prodigies are very advanced for their age, but their contributions to their respective fields as children are widely considered to be ordinary. It is not until they are older (and have practiced more) that they achieve the works for which they are known.

According to Willingham, athletes and artists revered by many students excel not solely by virtue of their talent but because of their hard work. Edison remarked that "genius is one percent inspiration and 99 percent perspiration." The relative percentages of talent and practice are unclear, but the necessity of long periods of focused practice to exploit inborn talent is not.

Courage to find strength through pain and failure

Courage is another lesson we learn from failing. Courage of the type envisaged here is of one of two variants: the first is the courage to admit wrong, which then allows us the insight to make necessary corrections to find our way, and the second variant is the courage to take a hit and not allow the fear of it or the shock of it to deter us from our allotted path. The impediment is that an inability to admit when we are wrong is directly tied to a lack of humility, which may have us on a path that we know at a certain level is also wrong, as we are now placing ourselves in alliance with people, concepts, and circumstances over our ultimate objective, betraying our overall ambition. This occurs merely because we cannot face the shame or embarrassment of disrupting those relationships. Another possible impediment may be that we are so afraid of the consequence of being wrong and the pain and suffering of correcting our course that we stay on the wrong course, hoping and wishing things turn out for the best but lacking the courage to ensure that they do.

A principle referred to as path dependence. To say that "when we know better, we do better" is predicated on the notion that "all knowing is doing and all doing is knowing," and thereby, that knowledge is expressed in how we live. However, this appears to be moderated by a set of competing interests that may cause a conflicting stream of thought and action where we are more tied to our past habits, relationships, practices, emotional connections, and such. We are loyal to who we were more than who we are becoming or what we think best for ourselves at any given point in time. We know to eat vegetables and go to the gym and that a penny saved is a penny earned, but we still don't work out, eat right, or save for a rainy day. This competing interest is the issue. There is a stronger connection to what's familiar to us, notwithstanding whether or not it is good or bad for us, which makes no difference. It is here we must apply the humility to admit we may have been wrong, have the courage to break those ties to free ourselves from that competing interest, and act in accordance with what we know is best for our lives. It is here we must exercise the courage to accept and admit wrong and chose to move in a more advantageous direction, which takes a great deal of emotional strength. This issue for most of us is that corrections have severe consequences. This requires the courage to change course and the courage to withstand the consequences of following your knowledge, whatever it may be. This is the courage to take the hit, the pain, and discomfort of your allotted decision and not be afraid of that pain associated with your commitment to that change. Doing better is not always easy as more often than not, what thrust us in this direction is when we get into trouble or are under a threat. Or even when in competition, we become motivated to change. Knowing better does not always mean doing better, but it is impossible to do better without knowing better. The complexity of this competing interest comes when we learn something new and decide in our best interest to apply it in our lives whether it be to lose weight, get a better education, go into a particular line of work, pursue a particular relationship, etc. We are often deep into our present circumstances and maintain relationships, commitments, and obligations as we currently are, which must be disrupted when we realize these commitments are not going to get us where we want to go. In contemplating a change of any kind, we become aware of the disruption and are confronted with a choice: do I continue to endure the pain of inertia of staying the course of prior decisions, or do I make the change and suffer the immediate and often short-term pain of breaking the inertia, diving into the uncertainty of where I am trying to go? We became stuck in a situation we helped create and feel guilty that we must move, however, knowing that someone will get hurt in the end. Correction will have severe consequences, similar to sunk costs in business. We made decisions in life, and now we know better but are stuck with the consequences of those past decisions. This is the competing interest that prevents us from doing better when we know better. This requires courage and emotional strength to overcome, which takes the form of humility to change. This is because at such times, no matter what we choose, there will be pain—either the pain of those lost connections and relationships or our own personal pain of lost ambition to be become better.

Concurrent with my military enlistment, I got married. I was nineteen years old and had just found that I was having twins. I was then in the singles dormitory on base, sitting in the phone booth down the hall from my room. To be totally honest, I worked myself up to be ready for the news of one child, only to find out that I was having twins—as a teenager. Here, I had joined the Air Force to get my life in order and instead, carried my poor judgement with me across country. They do say, however, "Everywhere you go, there you are." I should explain. I joined the Air Force after dropping out of college, or should I say failing out, and breaking up with my then girlfriend, Michelle (the high school sweetheart and soon-to-be wife). However, a month after arriving at basic training, I found out that we were pregnant. I decided to do the responsible thing and we got married and moved her to California with me. Enlisting and getting married was a last-ditch attempt at pulling it all together. Needless to say, necessity doesn't always foster great relationships. Things did not go well for us over the next three years as we fought constantly and broke up a number of times with one time Michelle moving with the kids back to New York. My time with the Air Force came to an end during the time we were apart, and I moved in with an old friend from high school who was attending a local university. I slept on his floor for a while, while I got myself together. An opportunity came for me to join a regional broker dealer as a sales assistant to the president, and I thought, *Wow, maybe this is a good time to try reconciling with my wife.* I always thought our troubles were the result of my struggles alone—arrogance on my part. Subsequently, due to my early success, I moved on to the, then, number two broker dealer,

Shearson Lehman Brothers in Berkeley California. We got back together, moved to Richmond, California, and bought a new car. Things went well for a time but then inevitably broke down for the last time as far as I was concerned. Fearing that having become a broker before completing my undergraduate degree was my big break, I would see to it that nothing would interfere with my new career. I was also exhausted physically and emotionally from the constant discord and police visits to my home. So I moved out presumably for the last time, but only thirty minutes away to San Leandro so I could stay close to the kids. On my birthday of that year, Michelle and I had lunch as she also worked nearby in Berkeley for the university. During lunch, I noticed she was not doing well, as often was the case. She was agitated and erratic as she advocated for the relationship to continue hobbling along as it had been over the past few years. I promised myself that after the third separation, I would call it quits because it was just too emotionally draining and disruptive to both of us overall. I just could not continue this painful experience at the expense of the remainder of my life and ambition. I had to stand my ground and put an end to this relationship. That evening, she left me a rambling, meandering voicemail, offering farewells to everyone and leaving me to wonder where she was going. Part of me was angry.

For as long as I had known her, she was prone to making suicidal threats when things didn't go her way. But still, I would show up at the house that evening to continue the conversation and hope to talk sense to her. She was nowhere to be found—no car, no Michelle. It didn't seem too unusual for a Friday evening. Two days later, I got a call from my mother in New York to inform me that Michelle was in the hospital from an apparent suicide attempt. For the next week, I sat by her side in a Richmond hospital as her brain activity slowly diminished, and she slipped away. My mother arranged for my aunt to fly out, support me, and ultimately give the order to remove her from life support.

Since that time, I have replayed those events over and over in my mind as to what I could have done differently. Was it my fault? Did I do the right thing, standing my ground in leaving the relationship? This illustrates the earlier point about taking thoughtful action that, although might hurt some in the near term, provides a permanent solution, with both options being equally painful. I just could not bear more breaking up, getting back together, and losing sleep and opportunities due to incessant bickering and arguing about nothing. I could not take doing "Now you see me, now you don't" to my kids anymore. In retrospect, yes, I did the right thing in drawing the line. Realizing the dysfunctional and dire nature of the situation, I made the decision for the sake of myself and the well-being of my children. Too often we tend to imprison ourselves in this form of regret and ambivalence when faced with difficult decisions all the while knowing better but choosing to do nothing. At the time, I felt my livelihood was in jeopardy and that I did all that I could in the given situation. Painfully, I had to move on and continue to focus on the broader well-being of all of us. All too often, we stick with the devil we know—decisions we made in the past but now, with more knowledge, we must live with the consequences of those choices or endure the pain of changing course. In retrospect, we become stuck in decisions made out of bad information, immaturity, discontentment, selfishness, restlessness, emotionalism, pride, etc. Now that we know better, we are left unable to do better. Negotiating this requires courage and humility to admit we were wrong and emotional strength to correct it. Humility enough to quiet the ego enough to bring about change, else the disruption that comes with the decision to change will cause us to become trapped in regret.

Oftentimes, humility is required in order for us to declare, "I was wrong and now must take a new direction." The problem is that most of us are ill equipped and lack such humility to act in this way.

In our weakness, we too often become loyal to the mistake as we are afraid of correcting the mistake because it comes with great disruption for others while we think we can just carry the pain instead. As such, we become stuck as we hate our normal but fear the uncertain and the pain of change. However, we must understand the importance of change and exercise the humility it takes to understand that we were wrong as until we take responsibility for the mistakes made in the past, we will never transcend these circumstances. In order to move forward, we must let something go—cut something from the program, cast some things away, and say goodbye: "You helped me get here, but although you can go no further, I must go on to complete my journey. And to you I must now say goodbye." Idries Shah (1971), in his book *The Sufis*, demonstrates this with a short story of an island somewhere and its inhabitants. The people long to move to another island where they could have a healthier and better life. The problem was that the practical arts of swimming and sailing had never been developed or may have been lost long before. For that reason, there are some people who refuse to think of alternatives of life on the island whereas others intended to seek a solution to their problems locally without any thought of crossing the waters. From time to time, some islanders reinvented the arts of swimming and sailing. Also, from time to time, the student would come up to them, and the following exchange would take place:

"I want to swim to another land."

"For that you have to learn how to swim. Are you ready to learn?"

"Yes, but I want to take with me my ton of cabbages."

"What cabbages?"

"The food I'll need on the other side or wherever it is."

"But what if there's food on the other side?"

"I don't know what you mean. I'm not sure. I have to bring my cabbages with me."

"But you won't be able to swim with a ton of cabbages. Its's too much weight."

"Then I can't learn how to swim. You call my cabbages weight. I call them my basic food."

"Suppose this were an allegory and, instead of talking about cabbages we talked about fixed ideas, presuppositions, or certainties?"

"Humm...I'm going to bring my cabbages to someone who understands my needs" (Shah, 1971)

The little islander in the foregoing story is afraid of the unfamiliar and lacks to courage to trust in what lies ahead even though he has limited conscious awareness of where the cabbages came from in the first place. He is refusing to let go of the past and the known, not realizing this is what's required to move on. Letting go of what's familiar is difficult but equally necessary in order to make effective changes in our lives. An abundance of humility enables us to accept the consequences of correction, allows us to accept the pain of our decision, and affords us the ability to move forward with courage. Historically, we are enamored by those who had the humility and courage to change course and act under their conviction in the face of threat and adversity.

Courage to admit we are wrong and changing course

Why is it so hard to admit when we're wrong? Why do certain people find it almost impossible? Such a disposition is in itself problematic, and it can be very serious in today's society, where we've all seen examples of powerful people who never ever admit to making a mistake even when they're demonstrably wrong. For example, former POTUS Donald Trump is one of the least humble people on the planet. It was Trump who said on the night of his nomination, "I alone can fix it," with the "it" being our entire political system. It was Trump who once said, "I have one of the great memories of all time." More recently, Trump told the Associated Press, "I have a natural instinct for science," when dodging a question on climate change. A frustration about Trump and the era of history he represents is that his pride and his success—he is among the most powerful people on earth—seem to be related. He exemplifies how our society rewards confidence and bluster, not truthfulness. Yet we've also seen some very high-profile examples lately of how overconfident leadership can be ruinous for companies. Look at what happened to Theranos, a company that promised to change the way blood samples are drawn. It was all hype, all bluster, and it collapsed. Or consider Enron's overconfident executives, who were often hailed for their intellectual brilliance. They ran the company into the ground with risky, suspect financial decisions. The problem with arrogance is that the truth always catches up. Trump may be president and confident in his denials of climate change, but the changes to our environment will still ruin so many things in the future.

The bottom line is that for some people, conceding that they're fallible can evoke a deep psychological anxiety regarding the risks or the consequences associated with loss or failure. Dr. Tim Sharp, chief happiness officer at The Happiness Institute, explains, "I think the reason some can't apologize isn't actually because they don't like to be wrong but because it's seen as an inherent character fault." He says that for those who refuse to apologize, the irrational need to always be "perfect" rules their ego, and they feel their mistakes are unforgivable. "The difficulty in admitting failure largely comes from the unrealistic expectation that 'I should get it right all the time,'" he says. These types of people believe never admitting fault makes you look stronger, but Sharp says they could not be more wrong because a good leader always admits their mistakes. "There's some actually very interesting research that leaders who express vulnerability and are more open to being fallible tend to be more highly regarded," he adds. Leaders with a deep sense of accountability can inspire people to think of them as deeply trustworthy and inspire higher levels of engagement and productivity.

The opposite of this intellectual arrogance or conceit is intellectual humility. Simply put, it resembles open-mindedness. Intellectually humble people can have strong beliefs but are able to recognize their fallibility and are willing to be proven wrong on matters both large and small. Intellectual humility includes an awareness that one's beliefs may not be right. The trait has only recently begun to be studied by researchers. Yet this characteristic may influence people's decision-making abilities in politics, health, and business. It is important to provide grounding on what humility is before analyzing its components. Some have defined humility as a relatively stable trait that is grounded in a self-view that something greater than the self exists. Humble individuals do not have strong needs to self-enhance or to dominate others. Humble individuals understand their own strengths and limitations accurately and possess an openness that appreciates the views and contributions of others. Humble individuals are not self-deprecating; they recognize their strengths, admit their mistakes and weaknesses, and assume their role with others in a broader community. It is this kind of humility that is an essential component in the kind of courage it takes to make corrective actions necessary to change course at times when needed.

For example, science is often hailed as a self-correcting enterprise. In the popular perception, scientific knowledge is cumulative and progressively approximates truth more accurately over time. However, errors can persist for decades, corrections sometimes reflect lucky accidents rather than systematic investigation and can themselves be erroneous, and initial mistakes might give rise to subsequent errors before they get caught. Julia Rohrer (2018), a personality psychologist at the Max Planck Institute for Human Development, is trying to get her peers to publicly, willingly admit it when they are wrong. To achieve this, she and others started the Loss of Confidence Project. This organization seeks to address the questions of "To what extent does our research culture resemble the self-correcting ideal?" "How can we facilitate such behavior?" and "How to gauge the potential impacts of individual self-corrections?" It was designed to be an academic safe space for researchers to declare for all to see that they no longer believe in the accuracy of one of their previous findings.

Rohrer stated, "I do think it's a cultural issue that people are not willing to admit mistakes," and said that her "goal is to gently nudge the whole scientific system and psychology toward a different culture" where it's okay, normalized, and expected for researchers to admit past mistakes and not get penalized for it. The project is timely because a large number of scientific findings have been disproven or have become more doubtful in recent years. Intellectual humility is simply "the recognition that the things you believe in might in fact be wrong," according to Mark Leary, a social and personality psychologist at Duke University. Intellectual humility, however, should not be confused with overall humility or bashfulness. It's not about being a pushover, and it's not about lacking confidence or self-esteem. The intellectually humble don't cave every time their thoughts are challenged. Instead, it's a method of thinking. It's about entertaining the possibility that you may be wrong and being open to learning from the experience of others. Intellectual humility is about being actively curious about your blind spots. One illustration is in the ideal of the scientific method, where a scientist actively works against her own hypothesis, attempting to rule out any other alternative explanations for a phenomenon before settling on a conclusion. It's about asking, "What am I missing here?"

It's a common misconception that showing humility will make you an ineffective leader. In actuality, humble leaders make more informed decisions, create high-performing teams, and increase employee engagement. These outcomes are crucial to implementing change within organizations. Let's take a closer look at how leading with humility creates the conditions that generate better results when executing change. As illustrated by the Loss of Confidence Project, if you have humility, you understand that you can be wrong and don't have all the answers and are open to other people's ideas and viewpoints. It enhances critical thinking skills by overlooking the ego of being right and instead helps you explore options and opinions that differ from yours. In fact, researchers at Duke University found that people who possess intellectual humility have a higher ability to assess the quality of information they receive. As a result, you utilize the strength, knowledge, and input of others on your team to make better decisions. There's a reason why we get annoyed when leaders surround themselves with yes-people. We want leaders who like to have their viewpoints challenged, and you can only do so when you let go of your pride.

It doesn't require a high IQ or a particular skill set, but it does, however, require making a habit of thinking about your limits, which can be painful. It's a process of monitoring your own confidence. When you share your mistakes and talk about how you conquered your fears, you're educating your employees about your growth process. As employees hear the ups and downs of your experience, their own growth is validated, and it's easier for them to identify their own mistakes. According to a study published in the *Academy of Management Journal*, this shared sense of humility or collective psyche has added value because it fosters an environment of learning that emphasizes improvement and evolution. When employees concentrate on their growth and development, their interest in their work expands, and their engagement goes up. Most important of all, the intellectually humble are more likely to admit it when they are wrong. Acquiring intellectual humility isn't easy, but it's a quality worth striving for. It doesn't mean we have to give up on the ideas we love and believe in. It just means we need to consciously choose those ideas, be open to adjusting them, seek out their flaws, and never stop being curious about why we believe what we believe.

Courage to take the hit

The second type of courage required is in understanding how to take a hit and keep going. The promise of practice is resilience in the face of adversity. If you persevere, you will overcome, but you will also take some hits along the way. The issue is how does one get used to taking blows and not shut down as a result? In 1985, Richard Strozzi-Heckler was invited to contribute to a US Army Special

Forces project designed to test the effectiveness of integrating various practices into its training program. During the six-month program, he taught aikido and meditation techniques. His course incorporated the philosophy and teachings of the Shambhala warriors of Ancient Tibet, the American Indians, the Japanese Samurai, Zulu warriors, and others. Among his many lessons, he taught that these historical and mythical warriors found their strength and integrity by defeating their own inner demons, living in harmony with nature, and serving their fellow man. He operates on the belief that if we embody the virtues of these archetypal warriors, we're acting in support of the whole planet instead of constantly fighting external enemies for petty ends, and that the warrior power arises from a source that does not rely on a sexual hierarchy or, for that matter, any hierarchy. It's a power of self-knowing, self-educating, and self-accepting from trends or tyrannies, including gender and race. The warrior is connected with him- or herself. And only from that connection does he or she connect to others and the environment. The urge to confront personal ghosts and uncover our full potential is ignited only by an inner need. This arises from a discontent about who we have become. When the need becomes strong enough to challenge the status quo, we summon the commitment and courage to attempt the unknown. In order to face the demons that arise when we move past the boundaries of our small self, we need precisely the courage of our commitment to move us forward. If we do not have this commitment, its altogether too easy to say it hurts or is uncomfortable and then return to our smaller self. If we do not feel this inner need and commitment to change, we may be headed for rough seas.

Heckler emphasizes the principles of centering, blending, grounding, and how to use our *ki* (or energy), as the foundation and *ukemi* (the art of attacking and falling). Although his students may fear hurling their bodies over one another, the real challenge is to slow them down so they'll feel their movements and not simply perform them. Heckler explains that in ukemi, you learn how to give up your ground without giving up your center. The difference being that the center is the connection with one's own sense of personal power. To be grounded is extending that power into the environment. For example, imagine yourself standing on a well-polished marble floor, and you have wool sweat socks on. You can be centered but not too well grounded. Take the sweat socks off, and you can ground yourself. If I am thrown, I give up my ground. As I turn upside down in the roll, I can still keep my center—my own sense of personal power and choice. By learning how to do this on the mat, we can learn how to roll with any incoming energy or difficult situation without giving up who we are. This is critical to failing in any discourse as we sometime succumb to the fear of getting hit so much that it knocks us of track in the way of our performance, but understanding how to maintain our center and stay grounded helps us bounce back even quicker from the hit, shortcoming, or failing. Such methods equip us with strategies and tactics to further develop courage to overcome challenges on the mat as well as in life.

In discussing the courage to take the hit and press on in spite of it, the saying goes, "You don't have to fall off a log to know what it's like to fall off a log." Why get hit if you don't have to? Well, clearly, we all should avoid falling off the log, which is generally a good thing, but in life, we are going to take plenty of hits along the journey whether we like it or not. The best way to prepare for falling off the log is to fall off one. In a literal sense, it's hard to justify getting hit as a choice. Although we should prepare to block, bob, and weave away from getting hit because it's preferable not get hit if you don't have to, it's not always achievable. In fact, when it comes down to it though, getting hit is sometimes downright unavoidable. But what are benefits of getting hit? Well, first and foremost, fighting is meta-phorical. In life, we take hits, and the best way to prepare for them is to fall down. In this practice and acceptance, we find the inner calm that manifests itself in our outward self. Learning how to fall and get hit in and out of the ring has helped many find more peace of mind, more control of the body and breath, and more confidence.

This understanding is common among the surfers in a giant wave, the skier going all out on a downhill run, and the fighter in the ring, as the very best of them are relaxed while doing said activities. It seems incomprehensible that the most violent environments on earth could possibly create a sensation of being relaxed, but if you can look behind the violence, that's what you will see—rhythm and relaxation. How do they get there? Controlling one's breath is a big part, and swimming with the current is another.

It's interesting to note there are a lot of self-defense courses out there that mostly teach people offense, which, to many trained professionals, is comical and yet somewhat tragic. Self-defense means you have just fallen off the log. The first thing you need to prepare for is that fall—to take the hit in a protected way, which is only achievable by learning what it's like firsthand. Yes, it's true if someone has their hands on you, they are vulnerable and open somewhere on their body, and we have an opportunity for offense. But reacting in an offensive manner is not typically what happens. In this moment, we are often paralyzed with fear and as a reaction of just having been hit. Before the counter and the offensive response, we need to deal with the reality of what has just occurred. This comes from learning how to fall correctly. It starts with acceptance, and it ends with controlling the body and mind for breath and conserving our energy.

Learning how to get hit also means protecting ourselves by building a small shell around our bodies—hands up but in tight to the side of the body and head and, of course, chin down (a violent snap of the jaw is what creates the physiological reaction of a knockout). World champion boxer Bernard Hopkins would train with a small ball under his chin so he would keep his chin down and connected to his shoulder. It's bad for one's general posture but good for one's general defense. The key in creating our protective shell is to create one that is relaxed, effortless, and fluid. Rigid muscles, tension, and wasted energy are the enemy. Fighting is full of paradoxes, as is life—tight defense but not tense. Learning how to fall is perhaps the best way to know how to get back up.

One of the greatest aspects of martial arts is that you can learn many life skills while learning to defend yourself and engage in physical activities. Many of these life skills help establish a strong sense of self confidence, focus, and many other positive behaviors. One of the most important life skills you can have as a human being is understanding yourself well enough to truly know how you would react if someone tried to physically harm you. Many martial artists will never get the opportunity to be "pressure tested" in a safe and controlled environment, and instead, their first experience is in an unsafe attack on their well-being or possibly their life. This is a gross misstep on the part of any martial arts instructor and is in complete negligence of the student's safety.

Many martial arts schools limit their sparring to noncontact sparring or some other "safe" sparring in order to appear safer to the public and appear more marketable from a business standpoint. Noncontact sparring is absolutely the most unsafe type of sparring there is. One of the biggest reasons noncontact sparring is unsafe is that when you engage in noncontact sparring, you don't expect to get hit, which many times leads to someone leaving their guard down and not properly learning how to maintain a proper defense. Another problem is proper distance and timing can never be learned if you aren't experiencing the point of contact between you and your opponent. A student may get hurt because they get hit unexpectedly when moving in to attack, causing a clash. Another problem is that if you hit someone and you aren't used to the impact it causes, you can end up injuring yourself. You also hardly learn from your mistakes. When you make a mistake and the only consequence is a point awarded to your opponent, it has very little impact on you. If you get hit when you aren't expecting to, it is much worse than getting hit when you are ready and able to react appropriately. You might not have your mouth closed all the way, so you end up damaging your teeth or jaw. You might not be able to cover up with your defense in time. You might get hit in the body and not have the proper timing to flex your core muscles and breathe properly. You might be knocked off balance during any movement of your footwork.

Getting hit can be an incredible experience, especially for someone who has never really experienced it. When it comes to the effects of getting hit, pain is secondary to all the other things that happen to your body. When getting hit in the body, your breathing is disrupted, your balance is shaken, and you are temporarily immobilized; and getting hit multiple times in the body can make it difficult to maintain your stamina. This is why in boxing, it's called working the body. The goal of working the body isn't just to damage the body but instead to make breathing over time more difficult and cause your opponent to get exhausted. Getting hit in the face or head can really be a surprise when it comes to how it affects your body. If you've never been hit in the face, it is one of those things that is hard to understand what it's like unless you've experienced it yourself. Just like getting hit in the body, pain is not the main concern. Your eyes can water, causing blurred vision. Your balance gets thrown off drastically. Your nose may bleed, which can cause difficulty in breathing. Your attacks and footwork become interrupted. Your cheek or eyebrow may swell, obstructing your vision. You become jolted, almost like getting shocked by electricity. And of course, there is a chance of being knocked unconscious.

All these effects of getting hit may cause someone who has never experienced them before to react in a way that leaves them more vulnerable and overwhelmed. There are many incidents where somebody who was an experienced martial artist had to defend themselves for the first time, and they completely lost their composure. And all of their martial arts skills got thrown out the window. Their years of hard work and training were wasted because they didn't prepare themselves properly. They ended up panicking and scrambling in the fight like they had no skills at all. And many times, the fight did not turn out in their favor.

As mentioned earlier, getting hit has so many factors at play other than pain. If you ever get into a self-defense situation, the level of adrenaline that will most likely be flowing through your body will cover up most pain. There are neurological, psychological, cardiovascular, and other effects. These are the things that are most important in a fight. If you can't think, see, or breathe or if you get stunned, you will be at a major disadvantage in a fight. The key is to train yourself to be able to control these factors in any situation and to do it in a safe and controlled environment. It might be scary at first, but in the end, you will be a more complete martial artist. And you will be better prepared at defending yourself. When it comes to life skills, this type of training will teach you the most valuable self-defense skills you can learn from martial arts while greatly improving your character. Your focus, confidence, self-control, etc. will rise to levels you never thought possible. If you have the focus and confidence to handle a punch being thrown at your face, then you can probably handle just about anything life throws at you. As humans, all of our understanding and practices emanate from our central nervous system, so if we can physically endure extreme conditions, we can endure extreme psychological conditions as well as our bodies do not distinguish between the two. What is real is real, what hurts, hurts, and strength is strength. As it is in martial arts, it is in life. As undesirable as it may be, we all need the wisdom of taking the hit—understanding that the skills we learn in one discourse transfer to other aspects of life. Like Mike Tyson said, "Everybody has a plan till they get punched in the mouth."

The Rocky complex—know when to walk away and fight another day

On July 26, when it was unimaginable that Simone Biles would pull out of the 2020 Tokyo Olympics, it would have nonetheless been easy to predict the reaction in the United States. And as with so many things in America, opinion was often divided along political lines, so it came as no surprise that many saw Simone Biles as a villain. Since Biles's withdrawal from the team final and individual all around, many have rushed to her defense, agreeing that prioritizing mental and physical health is more important that competing for a medal. Initially, the immediate reaction to Biles's withdrawal was overwhelmingly positive, as *USA Today* called Biles's decision important and a powerful message. Biles certainly did not need to compete in the 2020 Tokyo Olympics. She has a combined total of six Olympic medals and twenty-five world championship medals. She has signature moves named after her that no other gymnast in the world can pull off. Still,

Biles traveled to Tokyo to compete after a years-long delay due to COVID-19 and not just to help her team rake in the medals: she came for fellow survivors. The *New York Times* lauded the twenty-four-year-old for putting her "mental health first and the expectations of others, at best, second." And after Biles spoke about the mental exhaustion endemic to being the best, the *Washington Post* asked, "What are we doing, breaking our athletes?" Making matters worse, Biles is a Black woman in a country facing a racial reckoning, where her gender still battles for equality in every arena of public life. She's also a survivor of abuse—a former patient of Larry Nassar, the disgraced Team USA physician who will spend the rest of his life in prison for crimes related to his sexual abuse of underage gymnasts. Earlier this spring, Biles revealed that she was dedicating her performance to sexual-assault survivors. She stated in an interview with Hoda Kotb of the *Today* show, "I feel like if there weren't a remaining survivor in the sport, they would've just brushed it to the side," as well as, "Black and brown girls over the world," as she told the *New York Times* in a phone interview. "At the end of the day, I am not representing USA Gymnastics." Biles is, in fact, the only victim of former Team USA gymnastics doctor Larry Nassar to represent Team USA. And while Biles went on to tell Kotb that the abuse she endured caused her to sleep "so much because, for me, it was the closest thing to death without harming myself," she still felt she had an obligation to return.

Biles explained to fans why she decided to gracefully exit by posting two videos of her training on bars, trying complete her twisting and flipping dismount. She explained that what she was supposed to do in the competition and what she actually accomplished in training did not match up. She said that in competition, she was supposed to do one and a half more twists than what she was able to do in training. "Almost there but not quite," she wrote, later adding, "Sometimes I can't even fathom twisting. I seriously cannot comprehend how to twist. Strangest & weirdest thing as well as feeling." Biles is also used to landing on a soft mat, which breaks the impact from a hard fall. On her Instagram story, Biles said she did not have a problem with her Olympic routine before she left the US for Tokyo. "It randomly started happening after prelims competition the VERY next morning," she wrote. "By that time NO an alternative was not allowed to be placed in my position for you 'know it alls.'

"We have four on a team for a reason," she continued. "I chose to not continue team competition in jeopardizing losing a medal (of any color) for the girls/US." When asked what it's like to experience the "twisties," which is the term for when a gymnast's air awareness is off, Biles remarked, "Literally cannot tell up from down. It's the craziest feeling ever. Not having an inch of control over your body. What's even scarier is since I have no idea where I am in the air, I also have NO idea how I am going to land. Or what I am going to land on. Head/hands/feet back... I didn't have a bad performance and quit. I've had plenty of bad performances throughout my career and finished competition. I simply got so lost my safety was at risk as well as a team medal."

For any gymnast, especially an elite one like Biles, air awareness is key as it means that at all times during a skill, they know where they are in the air and how long they have until they reach the floor. Biles admitted to having had the twisties before and had heard that they may be triggered by stress, but she was not sure that was what was happening to her that time. She also admitted that she didn't know how she made it through her vault routine, stating that she had no idea of how she landed on her feet on the vault because from one look at her eyes, you could see how confused she was as to where she was in the air. Biles stated, "Thankfully I landed safe enough but I also don't think some of you realize I was supposed to do a 2 1/2 and I only completed 1 1/2 twists before it looks like I got shot out of the air."

By choosing to withdraw to focus on her mental health and pri-
oritize her well-being, Biles reminded the nearly one in five women
and one in seventy-five men who are victims of sexual assault that
our stories, our bodies, and our minds do not need to be sacrificed
at the altar of social justice, that it's okay if we know deep in our
bones that we can't do what is required of us, that pushing through
would cause us harm, and that the pain, physical or not, simply
is not worth it. Despite her obvious burden and the fundamental
importance of mental health—which Biles, Naomi Osaka, and others have spotlighted—some have portrayed Biles's decision to withdraw not as a brave stand but rather as quitting in the face of adversity. However, the value of knowing when to quit, give up, or throw
in the towel was highlighted in a paper called "The Importance of
Goal Disengagement in Adaptive Self-Regulation: When Giving
Up is Beneficial" by Wrosch et al. (2003). These authors, referring
to quitting and giving up as goal disengagement, develop the argument that goal disengagement forms an essential aspect of effective
self-regulation. The authors present evidence to support the idea that
goal disengagement can be beneficial to psychological well-being. In
addition, the article addresses the nature of disengagement in that it
requires a person to withdraw not only effort but also commitment

from unattainable goals and is most adaptive if it leads to pursuing new meaningful goals. If ever there were a time to quit, this was it. Mental health is physical health. Your mind is not only within your body, but it is the captain of the ship. So if the captain of the ship says it's time to call it a day, you do what you're told. This Biles understands too well. Knowing her mind was not right, she was no longer willing to put her body in danger by continuing with this competition, so she withdrew. The unfortunate nature of sports is that we often expect athletes to win, but we dehumanize them in the process.

Early in my sales career, I was a student at the Aji Network in Sunnyvale, California. Toby Hecht, the program CEO, had once coined the term *Rocky complex*, which is where, in pursuit of our ambitions, we fail to know the right time to quit any given endeavor—where, in pursuit of our ambitions, we are taking an absolute thrashing and fail to know the right time to quit the task at hand before brain damage sets in or worse. All too often, we learn that no matter what happens in life, no matter how hard the ups and downs get, never give up! Even when it gets so difficult that it's hard to focus on achieving our goals and in the midst of all obstacles challenging our progress, it's possible to stay motivated even during the hardest times. This Rocky complex comes from those '80s Rocky movies about a boxer who sometime gets obliterated in the ring but somehow pulls it off in the end and secures the win, and sometimes he loses, landing himself in the hospital. The idea of a Rocky complex is akin to the Pyrrhic victory (winning the battle at the expense of everything else) but relates more to the interim experience.

However, in understanding that quitting may sometimes be in the interest of the greater good, the question remains: "When and why should we quit?" It has been suggested that we consider, among other things, whether the quest to solve a problem takes over all other aspects of our life, whether we feel that that we are not enjoying life to the fullest because we can't stop thinking about the given situation, or, as in the case of Simone Biles, the level of danger to our continued well-being and chance of injury increases with every step forward. If so, it might be time to reconsider the reasons we continue trying as our continued pursuit in this given direction may just be delaying better opportunities that may await us. Oftentimes, our quest to solve a problem is so pervasive that it takes over all other aspects of your life. If you feel that you're not enjoying life to the fullest because you can't stop thinking about your situation, this might be another instance to reconsider the reasons you continue trying. Working toward a worthwhile goal should be elating and exciting.

Lack of excitement about achieving what you think you want probably means that you've become used to "striving and never arriving." The striving is what you do; however, the routine no longer serves you. Also, you may be justifying a painful situation in the name of psychological comfort. Fear of the unknown or of upsetting other people could be the true driver of your efforts because perceived safety and popularity are comforting. What would your life be like if you stopped trying? Notice the first feeling that arrives when you ask this question. A feeling of freedom or exhilaration is a sign you are ready to give up. You aren't able to visualize a positive outcome. If you continue working to achieve a goal and yet it seems like an impossible dream to be successful, you'll sabotage your own efforts. In a quiet place, contemplate the realization of your goal in detail. Can you clearly picture the resolution of your problem? Can you see yourself succeeding and feeling good about your success? If not, it's a good idea to reassess your commitment to the goal. It's like dreaming about a fairy-tale ending to marriage or employment issues when the inner voice tells you there is a very small chance of success. The rational mind kicks in and even may find new reasons to keep trying. But this process of rationalization eventually makes you feel even worse about the possible outcome.

You start to feel poorly about yourself. Not being able to achieve your goal might result in self-doubt about your abilities. You might wonder whether there is something wrong with you. In most cases, a job, relationship, or project that hurts your self-worth isn't worth it. You're the only person who shows interest in solving the problem or reaching the goal, but the outcome also depends on other people. This is particularly relevant in relationships. If you are the only person who initiates contact with a friend or the only one who takes action to improve a relationship, it's unlikely that the relationship will thrive or even survive. Letting go of relationships in which you're the only person invested will produce temporary pain, but once you've overcome the negative emotions, you'll be able to welcome loving and uplifting people into your life. When you wake up in the morning, your first thought is to give up. You're most attuned to your intuition when you first open your eyes after a night of rest, and your intuition always knows what is in your best interest. The emotional pain required to silence the inner voice just is not needed or worth it. Trust that your intuition is guiding you to the places you're meant to go, the career you're meant to have, and the people you're meant to meet.

As a teen, I had a severe case of hoop dreams. I played basketball every day after school. I chased a basketball career at the expense of all else at the time and ended up not graduating from high school, which, in turn, dashed all hopes of my ever playing at the level I was training for. In hindsight, this was ridiculous, I know, but at the time, playing for an NCAA Division I college meant everything to me. I was stressed and anxious all the while, which affected my playing and my education. I chased the dream right up until it caused me to drop out of junior college. I didn't know when to let it go. The only thing worse than having no dream at all was accepting that the one you had is unattainable. So I finally quit only because it began to cost me my future. Could it have been that my motivation was being usurped by anxiety or fear of letting your friends and family down or even that perceived safety and popularity were comforting? I will never know definitively. However, if the first feeling you have when considering a change of direction is freedom or exhilaration, that may be a sign you are operating under the wrong motivation, as I was.

Lastly, sometimes failure really is failure, and we need to accept it for what it is. This requires that we face it honestly and avoid going too far to redefine it. Authors John Slocum, Cass Regan, and Albert Casey have argued that when CEOs fail, they frequently go through similar stages to those described in literature on death and dying: denial, anger, bargaining, depression, and acceptance. Notably, they often get stuck in the denial and anger stages. They refuse to take responsibility for their mistakes and frequently blame the mount attacks on others. As a result, they rarely reach the acceptance stage, which could open them to learning and renewed long-term success. In most situations that might have been called failure, they can be transformed into a stepping stone to success. But sometimes it's something else—real failure, and we need to face that we have failed—period. Until we do, we can find ourselves sinking deeper and deeper into darkness, tied to the past rather than rising toward a brighter future. Our long-term success may well depend on our accepting in the short run when failure is really failure.

To new beginnings

What may feel like an end may be just the darkness before the dawning of a new dream, a new challenge, a new opportunity, or a new tomorrow. You have the power within you to turn terminations into transitions. Nothing can appear as frustrating and overwhelming as having to start over again. The construction of the Panama

Canal will always be an inspiration to those of us facing challenges. If it were not for the leadership of Major General George Goethals and his willingness to start over again, it's possible that the Panama Canal project would have been abandoned and doomed to utter failure! Consider, for instance, the following incident: one section of the canal proved to be extremely difficult to dig out, and it took months of arduous work to excavate and build this one section, only to have it collapse. Imagine how disheartening that would be—surely a good enough cause to quit, pack up your bags, and go home! An aide shook his head in disbelief as he and the general stood and surveyed the damage. "What do we do now, general?" he asked. "Dig it out again," was his answer, and dig it out they did. Today, the world enjoys the benefits of this remarkable waterway.

Starting over may be the single most difficult time in your life. But never think that your efforts have been in vain or have been wasteful. You can learn from the experience, and nothing is more valuable than the education you gain from failing! If you're tempted to look at life in terms of cynicism and futility, just look out for your worst enemy—yourself. Have the courage to try and keep trying until you make your catch. T. D. Jakes says, "Everything you need to raise yourself is inside of yourself. You have the power inside of yourself to get up out of that situation and arise. It doesn't matter who didn't raise you, who didn't love you, who didn't teach you, who didn't help you, who didn't stand by you. Everything you need you got, everything you lost you do not. I will not pray about anything that you lost, but I will pray to strengthen the things that remain."

We must begin to embrace failure, understanding that the significance of that state of definitive failure is that we no longer have to worry about what other people think or that we have to face any more pain than we're already in. We can focus our attention with more deliberation and less hesitancy. With a platform below us, we can move with more clarity and more confidence. With less risk, we have the incentive to chase the reward more aggressively. It's not easy to think like this when we feel at our lowest. Feelings of inadequacy don't go away because we want them to, and that's okay. You just have to accept that you can either stay where you are or decide to be more. Failure can place limitations on our means by stressing our resources. If you're a business owner and you're dealing with low demand, you might be faced with a need for a new source of income. And until you're able to readjust, you may even have to downsize. It'll force you to live with less. In most developed countries, we live in societies of abundance, and after a while of getting used to that abundance, it can be easy to fall into the trap of thinking that less is bad. It's actually often the opposite of that.

The more we have and the more we have going on, the more complicated our life is. There's more noise, and there's less focus. It can be paralyzing. Barry Schwartz has analyzed much of the research on the topic. In *The Paradox of Choice*, he explains how backward our thinking on the concept is. He points out that although modern culture is obsessed with the freedom of choice, more choice isn't a good thing. Research has consistently shown that the more we have to choose from the less likely we are to do things.

3

SUCCEEDING THROUGH FAILURE

It's up to us what material we build the house out of, because we all will eventually get burned, and it's the fire that comes to reveal the material that we have been building with.

—Bishop TD Jakes, various sermons on YouTube

There are many high achievers that have confronted failure and bounced back to higher heights. Most, in fact, have come up against adversity at some point in their lives and, although having been felled by some sort of crushing defeat or another at some point, learned lessons that only failure can teach, which pushed them even closer to their ultimate objectives. The following personal stories offer some brief examples on how exactly they got past their setbacks to achieve success and highlights and the lessons they learned. By sharing their stories and early failures, the hope is to provide a closer examination on how failure can be converted to our advantage if we assume the proper perspective on our experience.

Ashley Good, environmental engineer

Ashley Good was born in 1983 in Toronto, Canada. She was described as a smart kid, but with that badge came the constant need to prove it—to herself more than anyone. Specialized in geophysics at UBC, she became "head of failure" for Engineers without Borders Canada in 2011 and started Fail Forward when she was twenty-nine. Fail Forward is the world's first failure consultancy and works to support people and organizations to allow, acknowledge, and adapt failure in pursuit of innovation. She claims to be globally recognized and has helped hundreds of individuals and businesses harness failure in order to learn, innovate, and build resilience. Good remembers a childhood spent poring over a workbook while her siblings played on their Game Boys and refusing to quit puzzles before she solved them. That drive led Good to score work right out of school, putting her environmental-science degree to use in Cairo at the United Nations Centre for the Environment then flying off to Ghana with Engineers without Borders. But all that success also left her ill-equipped to handle her first real brush with failure.

In 2010, Good was working for Engineers without Borders Canada (EWB) in Northern Ghana with a team, and although they were exceptional at their jobs, the project was failing in many ways for many reasons. She wanted to help boost the profits of women harvesting shea nuts in the region. She spent six months consulting with everyone from producers to exporters on a gourmet shea cooking oil, but when the then twenty-six-year-old pitched the idea to her supervisors, they simply shrugged it off. When the founder flew in from Rome to evaluate how the project was going, these brilliant people didn't feel safe talking to him about the real challenges and failures they faced every day. They liked their jobs and knew when he asked what wasn't working that it was safer to give standard answers like "Oh, we just need more time and funding" instead of ruffling feathers by talking about the embedded flaws in the project design. Watching this interaction play out, a light bulb went on for Good: projects would continue to be designed with these flaws until someone was brave enough to risk their good favor with the founder and tell them the truth about the challenges.

"In my naïveté, I assumed I had come up with something new,"
Good says. "But they'd already ruled it out." With her project shelved,
Good returned to Canada, only to be confronted with more failure
in her personal life: "I had just been dumped by the guy I thought I
was going to marry. I also didn't have a job," stated Good. She ended
up in her parents' basement in Toronto, wondering how it all went
south. "Life had been pretty easy up until that point," she says. "This
was the first time things didn't go my way." Good decided the best
way forward was to do something she was wired to resist: get really
cozy with the concept of failure. "Many of us grow up believing that
failure is an indicator of weakness," Good says. "That simply is not
true. As we take on harder challenges, failure becomes inevitable."
It's the way you get around those failures, she says, that helps you
improve as a person and an employee, building confidence, resilience, and an arsenal of hard-won lessons. She saw the same pattern
play out in many different sectors: CEOs of start-ups who knew the
company was struggling but didn't create the space for their staff to
talk about the deep flaws and failures, big companies with so much
success behind them that were unable to acknowledge the disruption happening to their industries, and government departments
that wanted to innovate and adapt to evolving needs of citizens but

couldn't rework the systems that reinforced the status quo. It occurred to her just how bad we all are at dealing with failure intelligently and how much this was (and is) holding our organizations back from the learning and adaptation required to stay relevant and competitive in a rapidly changing world. Months after her return home, Good was back with Engineers without Borders, working on a "failure report" designed to identify the organization's missteps and turn them into learning opportunities. *The Failure Report* was a publication dedicated to speaking openly about things that were tried and didn't work—past failures. Good made the report public, so it wasn't long before other organizations started calling to find out how she was able to create an organizational culture where openly talking about failure and learning was rewarded. As a side project, Good started consulting for these other organizations. And quickly, that little side project became bigger than her full-time job, so she made it her full-time job by starting Fail Forward in 2011. Two years after that, in 2012, she launched her own consulting firm, Fail Forward, to help companies adopt strategies for what she calls intelligent failure. Since then, Good, now thirty-one, has worked with Natural Resources Canada, Deloitte, and the Centre for Addiction and Mental Health, helping staffers get beyond the stigma of failure, embrace their mistakes, and learn how to fail better. "It's not failure we fear so much as being seen as a failure," she says. But accepting it as a natural part of success gives you permission to try something new.

Good jokes that she needs this work as much as anyone because even with the expert status she's achieved, she still struggles with a sense of inadequacy. It's a symptom of an incredibly common psychological phenomenon called imposter syndrome—the feeling that any day now, you'll be exposed as a fraud. Good attributes it to her fear that she's "not living up to [her] own standards of what [she] expect[s]." This is a very common sentiment. "People who feel like imposters experience shame when they fail," says Valerie Young, author of *The Secret Thoughts of Successful Women*. "They feel shame because they have an irrational, unsustainably high definition of what it means to be competent." While the syndrome's nagging effects are felt by both genders, women seem to bear the brunt of it partly because of their tendency to be hard on themselves. Young quotes a statistic from a Hewlett-Packard internal report: men apply for a job when they're only 60 percent qualified while women won't apply unless they have 100 percent of the credentials. Young points to studies that show that women are more likely to blame themselves when something goes wrong while men blame someone else.

Imposter syndrome is loosely defined as "doubting your abilities and feeling like a fraud." It disproportionately affects high-achieving people, who find it difficult to accept their accomplishments. Many question whether they're deserving of accolades. Imposter syndrome can be difficult, but it doesn't need to be paralyzing. Harnessing it starts by reframing your thoughts about failure: instead of wallowing, get motivated. For example, rather than beating herself up for not knowing answers to questions she's asked about failure, Good treats it as an indication of where her research should go next then returns to those questions frequently. That way, she says, "at least I can see myself getting better." It takes practice, she adds, but every time something doesn't seem to go well, "flip the idea of failure on its head." Good often reminds herself of something Albert Einstein said just before his death in 1955. "The exaggerated esteem in which my life work is held makes me very ill at ease," he said, "I feel compelled to think of myself as an involuntary swindler." Albert Einstein wasn't a fraud or a failure, and neither are you.

Good's Failure Report is a dynamic tool for learning, but the real power is its ability to shift organizational cultures. While producing the report is an accomplishment, measuring cultural indicators such as a hypothesis-driven approach to problem solving or a prevalence of celebrating risk is vital for building innovation into the DNA of the organization. If a CEO is willing to be a role model and admit his or her own failures or at least publicly reward those who are sharing their failures and learning, the adoption of the practice will be accelerated. Failure is an equalizer. The fact is that we all fail. Talking about it as peers, regardless of one's position, builds the empathy, trust, and safe space to continue doing so. Paradoxically, the most effective and innovative people and organizations are those that are willing and able to speak openly about their failures. Regardless, it is a challenging thing to do for just about everyone. To overcome this, Good has designed a workshop to encourage participants to think about their professional failures and then brainstorm what they would need to feel comfortable speaking openly about it. Investing the time to understand what your organization's existing context-specific bottlenecks are is a vital early step.

Among the many nuggets of Good's advice on failure is that we should decouple ego from activity. It is important to recognize that just because we may try something that fails, it does not mean we are a failure. Instead, we find a new kind of return on investment: the learning return. In times of failure, the return on investment or ROI is less than hoped for or lost entirely, and the goal becomes to maximize the learning return. In many cases, that learning can be just as or even more valuable in the long term if it is optimized and used to its full potential. This recognition allows egos to remain intact even in times of failure.

Additionally, we should tell stories. The tendency is to want to extract the lesson for people, parse them down, and take the context out to make the lessons widely applicable. But keeping the story intact allows readers to draw out the learning that is most relevant for their situation. What's more, the personality in stories makes the lessons more memorable and gives a platform upon which group discussion and interpretation can form. Other advice provided by Good is to "go big or go home," "No sugarcoating allowed," and maintain a dedication to honesty and humility as it is at the heart of making this work. Lastly, she admonishes that trying to euphemize failures as lessons learned or never tackling the tough failures and sticking to the no-risk variety undermines the cultural transformation needed for employees to dream big, take risks, and maximize the organizational potential for innovation.

According to Good, we all know in theory that we should take risks, innovate, and learn from and adapt to failures; but in practice, we tend to fear failure and deal with it poorly when it happens (i.e., ignore, deny, blame, self-criticize, try to fix it before anyone notices). And in doing so, we undermine our learning. As an example, Always #LikeAGirl research found half of Canadian girls feel society rejects those who fail, and eight in ten girls want to quit when failure happens. While lots of amazing thought leaders are talking about failing fast, building learning organizations, and prototyping, the focus should be on helping individuals and organizations change their day-to-day practices to turn the theory into action and create the conditions were failing intelligently is the norm.

T-Pain, R and B singer/songwriter

T-Pain was never very good at being a rapper. He tried to be when he was just starting out. It was said that he ultimately decided to break into hip-hop as a singer instead. The move worked: T-Pain's first album, Rappa Ternt Sanga, released in 2005, made T Pain, then only a twenty-five-year-old from Tallahassee, a star. T-Pain laughed a lot over the years, but he's been no stranger to voicing his mental anguish either. Featured in the recently released Netflix eight-part docuseries *This Is Pop*, T-Pain's comments about R and B superstar Usher elicited a round of spirited reactions. In the documentary, he recalled a 2013 conversation with the Usher aboard a flight to the BET Awards that T-Pain said sent him spiraling into a four-year depression. "Usher was my friend," T-Pain said. "I really respect Usher." Referring to his use of a technology called Auto-Tune, he recalled Usher saying, "Man, I'm gonna tell you something, man. You kinda f—ed up music." He continued, "I just didn't understand. I thought he was joking at first, but then he was like, 'Yeah, man, you really f—ed up music for real singers.'"

T-Pain became a sacrificial lamb for an element of the world of hip-hop and R and B that's still prevalent. The thirst for his music will likely never be what it once was two decades ago when he had one of the greatest runs of the 2000s. T-Pain didn't destroy the industry as Usher reportedly remarked, especially not one that notoriously creates and "swallows" artists to advance its own interests. Instead, T-Pain set the groundwork for an entire ecosystem and paid the price for it. T-Pain was at a point in his career where he had seventeen top-twenty hits on the Billboard Hot 100 between 2005 and 2009. What has caused him to be both revered and mocked was his use of Auto-Tune. Traditionally seen as nothing more than a pitch-correcting technology used in secret to patch up flawed vocal takes, Auto-Tune became something else in T-Pain's hands, turning the human voice into a new and bewitching instrument and giving his in particular a vaguely alien and a computerized quality that sounded at once triumphant and melancholy. Although it wasn't invented by T-Pain, he was next in line to become mightily successful because of it. Roger Troutman of the funk band Zapp famously used Auto-Tune's forefather, the Talkbox. Hits such as Jennifer Lopez's "If You Had My Love" and Cher's "Believe" later employed Auto-Tune's benefits to runaway success. T-Pain, however, brought Auto-Tune's abilities to the forefront in the world of hip-hop. Yet he was also the one whose career was blunted while artists that followed him—such as Nicki Minaj, Travis Scott, Quavo and Lil Uzi Vert—profited from his influence. One of them, Nicki Minaj, recently expressed remorse over turning down a chance to collaborate with T-Pain back in 2007. That's not a knock on them, but it is proof that trailblazers often burn up.

Everything about T-Pain was different from the moment he burst into the scene in 2005 with hits such as "I'm Sprung" and "I'm in Love with a Stripper." He never served as a spokesperson for trap music like T. I., Young Jeezy, or Gucci Mane or snap music like D4L and Dem Franchize Boyz were at the time. He also wasn't a part of the contentious guard like Kanye West, Lupe Fiasco, Little Brother, or Common. On top of that, he never identified with established gatekeepers such as Jay-Z, Nas, or Eminem. Lil Wayne and Ludacris might have been equally as rambunctious and prolific but never as happy-go-lucky as T-Pain always came off.

As unique as a three-piece suit at Mardi Gras, T-Pain was like the kid in computer class who was quirky and didn't fit the societal definition of what "cool" resembled. But his talent and penchant for infectious and, more importantly, fun smash records made him an in-demand artist. He gave hits to West, Lil Wayne, Plies, Jamie Foxx, Rick Ross, and more. But then everything changed. T-Pain went from being an in-demand artist to a novelty act. He hadn't gotten in trouble or gone to prison. The reasoning for this is simple. It's in part due to the industry and the trends that dictate it. The apparent collapse of his career sent T-Pain, now twenty-eight years old, into a depression that left him unmotivated to make any more music. Only recently has he emerged from this dark period: he has started work on a comeback album, landed the tense and pretty single "Up Down (Do This All Day)" on the charts, and today embarks on a tour called "I Am T-Pain." To promote all that activity, T-Pain has also been giving interviews, in which he has candidly discussed the experience of turning from one of pop's hitmakers into a walking punch line.

T-Pain was falsely credited for obliterating the art's purity. According to T-Pain himself, West wrote a diss track toward him while they worked on his 2008 Auto-Tune-heavy album *808s & Heartbreak*. And this was after T-Pain's appearance on their 2007 collaboration "Good Life," which peaked as a top-five song. Allegedly, West had everyone in the studio sing along, saying, "T-Pain s—is weak," a record even T-Pain admitted was good enough to put on the album, though it was never released. In 2009, Christina Aguilera donned a shirt that read "Auto-Tune is for p—ies," though she'd later recant that statement after using it on her 2010 album *Bionic*, saying she respected those who used it creatively.

Jay-Z's "D. O. A. (Death of Auto-Tune)" in 2009 all but sealed T-Pain's fate, though the song never mentioned him by name. It did, however, put him in the crosshairs. Due to the song's massive popularity, fans regularly chanted, "F—T-Pain," at his shows, prompting T-Pain to respond with "F—Jay." T-Pain later apologized, saying he had reacted emotionally. Artists such as Diddy and Fabolous called him "out of line" despite the obvious darts thrown at his direction. There were other attempts happening alongside this controversy that were obvious copies of T-Pain's style such as work released from Ron Browz, the Black-Eyed Peas, or The Game. Even Usher's 2010 hit "OMG" used Auto-Tune. And years later, T-Pain said Future's brother allegedly told him that "[Future] would never f—ing work with you. F—you and everything you stand for." That spat stemmed from T-Pain saying Future, who heavily used Auto-Tune as well, was "the next T-Pain."

"When I came out in the game, I was using Auto-Tune in order to make myself sound different. And then when everybody else started using it, it kinda made me sound the same again," he confessed on *Sway in the Morning* in 2013. "It's a bad thing to do, but I started telling myself, 'I was doing this for nothing …' It was just terrible self-esteem, basically." As a result, the buying public followed. His sales decreased dramatically, and radio play dwindled as well. T-Pain was an involuntary martyr, and he'd done nothing to bring about his own commercial demise. The entire ecosystem of the music industry did. "People can act like, you know, 'I don't care about when people hate on me,' but the second they do, you feel that!" he told the *New Yorker* in 2014. "Like, that's really somebody saying that s—about you. It's not, like, an artificially generated comment that these people are leaving on these YouTube videos. When people say I suck and I should kill myself, I don't really feel good about that!"

Not just in music but in many avenues of life, all too often, a person isn't given their proper due until it's too late. T-Pain is in search of the approval he believes his career deserves and not necessarily from fans. In the immediacy of his comments about Usher, a wave formed on social media to rush to his defense, but more so from his peers. Perhaps T-Pain, much like most artists, had simply run his course in his time atop music's mountaintop. It's just a shame that so many other powers made the decision for him.

Ultimately, T-Pain went on to sing live at an NPR special presentation in front of a small audience. He recounts how angry he was after the performance because he sang so well, according to fans who heard him on the Internet. Some of the comments only made him even angrier, as T pain recalls,

> *There wasn't, like, a vindication or anything like that, but there was a point. I don't know how, but I somehow got even more mad. I got more angry because it was such a surprise to everybody that T-Pain has an actual human voice... Like really, you all think my whole success was based off of software, like what? You gotta write good songs. You still*

gotta produce good beats. You still gotta do all these things, and you all are paying attention to this one "plug-in." It is so weird that it made me so angry that people like, "Oh my god, T-Pain can sing?" In one light, it showed how much people respected me more. In another light, it shows how much people didn't respect me before. So my philosophy, at this point, is to make myself happy. I just want to make music that makes me feel good, and if you don't like it, I didn't make it for you. And if you do like it, welcome to the club!

Michael Jordan, basketball

Most of us don't fail or succeed in the glare of a national spotlight, much less do it thousands of times with analysts endlessly critiquing every move. Perhaps that's why people love sports: they provide a black-and-white analogy for the gray backdrop of life. And no one has inspired more sports fans, young and old alike, than Michael Jordan. The story of Michael Jordan not making his high school team has been told and retold but continues to inspire with each retelling. In 1978, sophomore Michael Jordan tried out for the varsity basketball team at Laney High School. When the list was posted, Jordan's name wasn't on it. Instead, he was asked to play on the junior varsity team.

The reasoning behind the choice wasn't that Jordan didn't have enough talent or hadn't already distinguished himself as an outstanding basketball player. Rather, it came down to seniority, size, and a strategic decision: the varsity team already had eleven seniors and three juniors. That left space for only one more player, and the coaches chose another sophomore, Jordan's friend Leroy Smith. Smith was not as good as Jordan, but he added size to the team as he was 6'6" compared to Jordan's diminutive 5'10". What's more, the coaches knew that if Jordan had been chosen for the varsity team, he would play only when needed as a substitute for the more senior varsity players. On the junior varsity team, he would get more playing time and a chance to truly develop.

It was a perfectly logical choice for the coaches to assign Jordan to the junior varsity team for his sophomore year. But fifteen-year-old Jordan was devastated when the list was posted without his name. In his mind, it was the ultimate defeat—the ultimate failure. Jordan recalls, "I went to my room, and I closed the door. And I cried. For a while, I couldn't stop. Even though there was no one else home at the time, I kept the door shut. It was important to me that no one hear me or see me." Jordan was heartbroken and ready to give up the sport altogether until his mother convinced him otherwise. His relentless drive would lead him to break numerous records and become the most decorated player in the history of the NBA. He's credited with dramatically increasing the popularity of basketball both in the United States and internationally and inspiring the next generation of basketball players. After picking himself up off the floor, Jordan did what champions do. He let his failure and disappointment drive him to be better. He played on the junior varsity team, and he worked himself to the limit. "Whenever I was working out and got tired and figured I ought to stop, I'd close my eyes and see that list in the locker room without my name on it, and that usually got me going again." It became a pattern throughout Jordan's life that a disappointment or setback resulted in a redoubling of effort. High school rival player Kenny Gattison, who led his team to beat Jordan's team for the high school state championship, put it this way: "You got to understand what fuels that guy, what makes him great. For most people, the pain of loss is temporary. [Jordan] took that loss and held on to it. It's a part of what made him."

For most people, public failure becomes public humiliation, and that leads to retreat. Fear of public speaking is a good example. Few people are psychologically afraid of speaking their mind, and even fewer have physical speech impediments preventing them from doing so. Yet glossophobia, the technical term for speech anxiety, is consistently ranked among the most prevalent mental disorders, with a reputed 75 percent of the world's population experiencing some degree of anxiety around public speaking. Our fears have little to do with speaking, of course, and far more to do with the perceived impact and reaction that our audience may have. But for Jordan and elite performers like him, the fear of failure and public ridicule is transformed into a drive for success.

The pattern of defeat followed by success would follow Jordan to the University of North Carolina and later to the NBA. You can't think of the word *champion* without thinking of Michael Jordan, and there's no better proof that failure is simply a stepping stone to success.

Michael Jordan faced another formidable challenge decades later when he became the owner of the NBA basketball franchise the Charlotte Bobcats. Jordan had been a minority owner since 2006 but bought the majority stake from Bob Johnson in 2010. At the time, the business was hemorrhaging, so Jordan used his own money to cover the significant operating losses the team was experiencing. The first season was lackluster, but things got worse. In the 2011–2012 season, the team earned a mere seven wins alongside fifty-nine losses—the worst record of any team ever in the history of the NBA. In addition to—or maybe because of—their disastrous record, the Bobcats had poor community support. The Bobcats brand was synonymous with disappointment despite having one of the best basketball brands of all time at the helm—Michael Jordan himself.

But after the 2012–2013 season came to a close, Jordan started to turn things around. First, he brought in former Lakers assistant coach Steve Clifford to replace Mike Dunlap. In a change every bit as important as the new coach, Jordan agreed to remove himself from the process of managing the team's operations. Instead, Jordan focused on what Jordan can do better than anyone else: revitalizing the brand. He applied for and received permission to change the team's name to the Charlotte Hornets. Jordan himself became more involved in community events and forged a connection between the team and the city. The changes paid off. The team finished the 2013–2014 season with a winning record of 43–39, the second-best year in the history of the franchise. They even made it to the play-offs. At the same time, ticket and merchandise sales skyrocketed, and public opinion improved dramatically. The team was well on its way to making both a comeback and a profit.

Most of us look to successful people and assume they can do anything because of their past successes. The old joke about asking your doctor for stock tips comes to mind, as if just because you can cure an illness, you have wisdom about everything. Doctors don't make great stockbrokers, brain surgeons are horrible rocket scientists, CEOs aren't usually exceptional cooks, and basketball stars are rarely great baseball players (you can ask Jordan about that last one as well). Experience and knowledge are only valuable where applicable.

This mindset doesn't just fog our external lenses; it also blurs how we see ourselves. It is often hard for successful people to admit that they won't be good at something new. In Jordan's case, his basketball skills didn't translate into basketball management. It took some time, but Jordan certainly deserves credit for acknowledging what wasn't working and trying new things until he hit a winning combination. He gave up managing and focused on marketing—a skill he was uniquely qualified for. For Jordan, that became the recipe for success:

> *It's harder than most people think. Some people have been in this business a lot longer and still haven't put together a sustainable, successful scenario. When you make bad decisions, you learn from that and move forward. I think I'm better in that sense. I've experienced all of the different valleys and lows about ownership and the success of businesses. Does that constitute me being a better owner? Then I guess I am. Hard, yes, but flexing a new muscle is also exhilarating, especially when you eventually succeed…it's been fun. It's been hard, but I've had fun doing it.*

Steve Jobs, technology business

Steve Jobs was one of the greatest entrepreneurs of the last one hundred years. Not many entrepreneurs have double-unicorn entrepreneur status (i.e., they built two billion-dollar ventures in sales and valuation from scratch). Others in this group are Elon Musk, who is a triple unicorn, and Eli Broad, founder of Kaufman & Broad and SunAmerica. But even great entrepreneurs make mistakes, and we can learn from them. Jobs explains that while in college, he learned more auditing courses after he dropped out than when he was a fully matriculated student. The minute he dropped out, he could start taking course that interested him that he was unable to take before. He no longer lived in the dorms, so this was the time where he ate handouts at Hare Krishna temple and slept on a friend's floor. Such experiences with failure taught him to follow his intuitions. After Jobs withdrew from university, he took a calligraphy course because he could, and he learned everything about typography just because he was interested in it even though it had no practical application. It was in this course he learned everything about what makes great typography great. Later in life, this knowledge would be poured directly into the development of the Mac, the first computer with beautiful typography, according to Jobs. Through this experience, he relates that "you cannot connect the dots looking forward; you can only connect them looking backward." If he never dropped out, he would have never dropped into the typography class. Jobs said, "You must trust that the dots will connect in the future because believing they will eventually connect gives you to confidence to follow your heart even when it leads you off the well-worn path which has made all the difference…you have to trust in something: your gut, destiny, life, karma, whatever. Because believing that the dots will connect down the road will give you the confidence to follow your heart even when it leads you off the well-worn path. And that will make all the difference."

In 1985, however, less than ten years after he founded Apple, Steve Jobs was (essentially) fired. He was out. At age thirty, his life was flipped upside down, and he needed to move on from the only business he'd ever known. Jobs was forced to resign when CEO Jon Sculley felt Apple needed to reorganize and shift gears. He didn't see Jobs in the tech company's future plans. So he was gone—famously gone. It would take nearly twelve years before Jobs came back to the company that he started. Shortly after returning in 1997, Jobs took Apple into the stratosphere and completely revolutionized personal computers, handheld technology, and the way we consume information. We know Jobs today as one of the titans of tech, a giant of Silicon Valley, and a legend of the business. Yet the greatest lesson we can glean from the life of Steve Jobs is the very same one that he learned during his nearly twelve-year hiatus from Apple. The man we view as one of the most successful CEOs and leaders in business history profited most from an incredible, embarrassing failure. This failure profoundly impacted the way he thought and how he would innovate and use technology as his tool to change the way billions of people live. "I didn't see it then, but it turned out that getting fired from Apple was the best thing that could have ever happened to me," said Jobs.

During his time away from Apple, Jobs founded NeXT, a company that developed computer workstations, and later founded Pixar and helped the animation studio grow exponentially. He later became chairman and was an executive producer on the enormous hit movie *Toy Story*. Instead of sulking and letting that failure doom him, Jobs created an opportunity for reinvention and used his talents to grow two other organizations. Jobs really loved what he did and possessed the vision to create and innovate. He refused to accept second best. He refused to wallow in failure. He never settled. He worked each day with a subject matter that he cared about, which made it that much easier to talk about, market, and sell. Jobs was a marketing genius, and he was able to do so with such brilliance because he loved what he did. He came back better than ever because he knew that what he wanted to create for the world was a superior product that people would love.

> *Your work is going to fill a large part of your life, and the only way to be truly satisfied is to do what you believe is great work. And the only way to do great work is to love what you do. If you haven't found it yet, keep looking. Don't settle. As with all matters of the heart, you'll know when you find it.*
> *(Steve Jobs)*

For all the innovation, genius, and marketing expertise he brought to Apple, it was born from precious life lessons forged from challenges and adversity. Jobs ultimately became a very wealthy and successful man because he was forced to do some introspection and determine how he could get better. He never stopped innovating. This time, he took the lesson to grow both professionally and person-ally. He mended some of the personal relationships in his life, both with his previous partner and children. He later remarried during his time away from Apple and continued his evolution into becoming a more well-rounded man. He kept searching, kept looking, and made personal growth a lifelong quest. Jobs could have let getting fired from Apple define him for the rest of his life in a bad way. He instead took that moment and converted it into an exemplary model of growth. This is Jobs's greatest lesson and one we can all heed in our own lives.

Jobs ultimately had learned the importance of tempering his obsession with control, and he was much better at empowering his talented employees to do what they do best. Without a doubt, this change in his leadership style is a very significant contributing factor in Apple's return to the spotlight after suffering through some major setbacks during his absence from the company. Here are six of Job's greatest mistakes, all of which history shows he ultimately learned from.

Recruiting John Sculley as CEO of Apple. Feeling that he needed an experienced operating and marketing partner, the then twenty-nine-year-old Jobs lured Sculley to Apple with the now legendary pitch: "Do you want to sell sugared water for the rest of your life? Or do you want to come with me and change the world?" Sculley took the bait, and within two years, Sculley had organized a board campaign to fire Jobs. There is often a culture clash between strong-willed entrepreneurs and "professional" venture capitalists (VCs) or CEOs hired by the VCs. Professionals have a common language and a shared demeanor. Jobs was not liked and did not fit with the new culture of Apple's leadership. The board fired him. Jobs himself would surely consider hiring Sculley as a great mistake. Eventually, Jobs's demeanor and an internal power struggle over disagreements on philosophies between him and CEO, John Sculley, led to his ousting from the company. In Jobs's eyes, this event was devastating.

Believing that Pixar would be a great hardware company. When Jobs was the last and only buyer standing in 1986 when George Lucas had to sell off the Pixar graphics arm of Lucas Films (for $10 million), he never expected the company to ever make money on animated films. Instead, as Pixar historian David Price shows in his excellent book *The Pixar Touch*, Jobs believed that Pixar was going to be the next great hardware company. Not even a visionary like Steve Jobs could predict what unfolded at Pixar, yet to his great credit, he supported cofounders Ed Catmull and John Lasseter as they pursued their dream of producing a full-length digitally animated film from day 1. He protected their ability to make small bets on short films in order to learn how to eventually make a full-length feature film in *Toy Story*.

Not knowing the right market for NeXT Computer. Although Jobs tried to spin NeXT Computer as an ultimate success when the assets were sold to Apple in 1996 for $429 million, few in Silicon Valley agreed. The company struggled from the start to find the right markets and customers. If you haven't seen the video about Jobs describing the vision for NeXT's customers, you should watch it on YouTube. It's clear that even Jobs was confused. In it he says, "We've had, historically, a very hard time figuring out exactly who our customer was, and I'd like to show you why." Before eventually returning to Apple in 1997, Jobs went on to found NeXT and spin Pixar off into its own entity after purchasing the animated division of Lucas Films.

Launching numerous product failures. The Apple Lisa, Macintosh TV, the Apple III, the Power Mac G4 Cube, to name a few. Steve Jobs was brilliant about understanding how technology vectors were evolving, yet even he screwed up royally and often. The lesson that I take from these defunct products is that people will soon forget that you were wrong on a lot of smaller bets so long as you nail big bets in a major way (in Jobs's case, the iPod, iPhone, iPad, etc.). Jobs was a market research group of one at Apple, which carries with it great risk, yet it should be noted that his batting average improved over time, which comes as no surprise to those who study the benefits of developing strong creative muscles through deliberate practice.

Trying to sell Pixar numerous times. By the late 1980s, after owning Pixar for four or five years, Jobs tried on multiple occasions to sell the company just to break even on his investment, which ultimately equaled roughly $50 million. He shopped Pixar to, among others, Bill Gates, Larry Ellison, and numerous strategic partners and companies. No potential buyer bit. It was a good thing for Jobs and his legacy. He eventually engineered the sale of Pixar to Disney for $7.4 billion in 2006. Once he returned, he led the charge on Apple's new OS, which redefined how personal computers function, the iPod, which completely revolutionized the music industry, and the iPhone, which has been equally as important in the evolution of personal technological devices.

Appointing Tim Cook as successor. Luckily for Jobs, all the CEOs between Jobs I (his first run at Apple) and Jobs II (when he returned to lead Apple from the abyss of doom) were not suited to the task. When Jobs returned, he pulled off one of the greatest comebacks and turnarounds in history. And when he departed from Apple and from the world, he left Tim Cook in charge. The problem was that even a talented unicorn entrepreneur would have had a tough time matching Jobs's exceptional talent at finding the next great emerging industry and dominating it. Tim Cook is showing us that he is a professional CEO who can explain why Apple has problems (with China, with his suppliers, and with the new models) but has not introduced a single new billion-dollar unicorn businesses along the lines of the iPod, iPad, and iPhone. The old businesses are mature, and competitors have caught up. Should the board of Apple and its shareholders, demand more?

The lesson, it seems, is fairly simple: even the great business visionaries and luminaries of our times often fail and have setbacks. Imperfection is a part of any creative process and of life, yet for some reason, we live in a culture that has a paralyzing fear of failure, which prevents action and hardens a rigid perfectionism. It's the single most disempowering state of mind you can have if you'd like to be more creative, inventive, or entrepreneurial. The antidote is to try a small experiment, one where any potential loss is knowable and affordable.

Although Steve Jobs is no longer with us, he truly changed the world with the products he helped shape and lessons he imparted along the way. As an entrepreneur, Jobs taught us that it is challenging for a leader to be successful if they're too reckless or unshakable in their way of thinking. This intense drive for perfection often leads to the failure of young technology companies, which should be focusing much more seriously on validating their core product offerings as opposed to perfecting them straight out of the gates. Leaders do need to take risks along the way, pushing for the results they want to see in business while also accepting that there will be failures at times. In the case of Jobs, he didn't allow his initial failure at Apple to define his life. He went on to learn from his experiences, create more businesses, and eventually return to help make Apple great again. Embracing his failure gave him the motivation to move further forward. Jobs recalls that none of this would've happened if he was never fired from Apple.

Chris Gardner, financial services

The story of Chris Gardner was chronicled in one of the most inspiring movies in present-day history: *The Pursuit of Happyness*, starring Will Smith, in 2006. Gardner wrote his autobiography to shed light on his early struggles and failures in life, which resulted in an immense amount of pain. Born in 1954, Gardner had a rough upbringing. With a father that wasn't present, his mother and siblings suffered abuse at the hands of his stepfather. In and out of the foster care system, Gardner was at the mercy of an unstable childhood. In 1977, Gardner married Sherry Dyson. But after a three-month affair with another woman who became pregnant with his child, he decided to leave his first wife. In 1981, his son, Christopher Gardner Jr., was born while he was working as a research lab assistant at UCSF, which didn't pay enough to help support his family. This led to the decision to become a medical-equipment salesman. It was back in the early 1980s that Mr. Gardner, then aged twenty-seven, and his toddler son were homeless for a year in San Francisco. However, this all changed dramatically when he met a random stranger driving a red Ferrari who ultimately led him on a career path to become a stockbroker. Now enrolled in a commission-based trainee program at the stock brokerage firm Dean Witter Reynolds (DWR), he didn't have enough money to raise the deposit to rent an apartment, resulting in Mr. Gardner, who was estranged from his partner, and Chris Jr. to instead sleep wherever they could. In addition to the toilet at a railway station, they'd bed down in parks, at a church shelter, or under his desk at work after everyone else had gone home. They ate in soup kitchens, and what little money he had was spent on putting his son in day nursery so he could go to work. Gardener struggled but was committed to living a better life, one that didn't involve so much struggle and turmoil. During his journey, he suffered through an eviction and homelessness, jail, and an eventual divorce. But that didn't stop him, not whatsoever. Despite all the adversity, Mr. Gardner thrived in his job. He was a natural at selling stocks and bonds; and at the end of his training period, his firm, DWR, made him a full employee. After he was finally able to rent a home for himself and his son, his career then rapidly ascended into the stratosphere, and in 1987, he opened his own investment firm, Gardner Rich. Today Mr. Gardner, sixty-two, is worth an estimated $ 60 million (£48 million), travels the world as a motivational speaker, and sponsors a number of homeless charities and organizations that combat violence against women.

Looking back on his life, Mr. Gardner tells *BBC* that he wouldn't change anything. "I went through pain as a child so my children wouldn't have to," he says. "I made a decision as a five-year-old boy that my kids will know who their father is. The most of my important decision that I ever made in my life was that my children would always know who their father was." In his autobiography, Gardiner says,

Without knowing the names, circumstances, or social conditions, I consciously chose to break every cycle that I was born into. Child abandonment, Child abuse, alcoholism, domestic violence, fear,

poverty, and illiteracy. The second-most-import-
ant decision that I ever made in my life was that I
would become WORLD CLASS *as whatever I did in my*
life. This decision led me to a career on Wall Street.
In fact, 30 years in the financial services industry
and wouldn't trade a day of it for anything in the
world. I'd also never go back… A very big part of
what I want to do with the rest of my life is simple;
I want to help create the next "Chris Gardner."

The message is equally simple: "If I can do this, then you can do that."

Michelle Wie, golf

If you have never heard of Michelle Wie, it's most likely due to the fact that she experienced crushing failure and defeat in her aspirations during the midpoint of her journey in golf. Born on October 11, 1989, in Honolulu, Hawaii, she is the only child of immigrant parents from South Korea who came to the United States in the 1980s. Michelle is an American professional golfer who plays on the

LPGA Tour. At age ten, she became the youngest player to qualify for a USGA Amateur Championship. Wie also became the youngest winner of the US Women's Amateur Public Links and the youngest to qualify for an LPGA Tour event. She turned professional shortly before her sixteenth birthday in 2005, accompanied by a great deal of publicity and endorsements. She won her first and only major at the 2014 US Women's Open. As a kid phenom, Wie had a handful of top-five finishes in majors but never won one. After turning pro at sixteen, she went years without winning any LPGA title, period. Wie's career has always had this push-pull feel to it. At twenty-five years old, with eleven years on tour behind her as an amateur and pro, her career was among the most eventful, even controversy-filled. Wie was derided as being famous for merely being famous. Wie's parents—who were born in Seoul, South Korea, and moved to Honolulu before their only child was born—were accused of having a bad case of stage-parent-itis. Both Michelle and her parents will admit now that they made mistakes. Michelle's father, a professor at the University of Hawaii at Manoa, had studied Tiger Woods extensively. He even carried a wallet photo of Woods swinging a driver, which he consulted if Michelle's swing broke down while he caddied for her or when they practiced on the range. Michelle's mother, Bo, was a single-handicapper who taught her husband the game. Early in her career, Wie employed many different caddies after her father stopped being her caddie in 2004.

In 2000, at the age of ten, she became the youngest player ever to qualify for the US Women's Amateur Public Links Championship. At eleven, Wie was hailed when she missed qualifying for the PGA Sony Open at the Pearl Country Club in Maui by a mere stroke. Later, a golf writer would call it the "worst thing that ever happened to Wie's career" because it encouraged her to keep chasing the cut at men's tournaments. In 2002, she won the Hawaii State Open Women's Division by thirteen shots. She also became the youngest player to qualify for an LPGA event: the Takefuji Classic held in Wie's home state of Hawaii. While she went on to miss the cut, her record stood for five more years until it was broken in 2007 by eleven-year-old Ariya Jutanugarn. At the 2003 Kraft Nabisco Championship, Wie became the youngest player to make an LPGA cut. In June 2003, Wie won the Women's Amateur Public Links tournament, becoming the youngest person ever, male or female, to win a USGA adult event. Later that summer, she made the cut at the US Women's Open when she was still just thirteen—the youngest player ever to do so. Wie, after having been given a sponsor's exemption to the 2004 Sony

Open in Hawaii, becoming the fourth and youngest female to play a PGA Tour event, had the lowest score ever by a woman in a PGA Tour event. At age sixteen, two years later, she committed amateurish mistakes like failing to sign scorecards or not knowing the rules of golf. On October 5, 2005, a week before her sixteenth birthday, Wie announced that she was turning professional. She signed sponsorship contracts with Nike and Sony reportedly worth more than $10 million per year.

Wie played her first professional event in the 2005 LPGA Samsung World Championship, where she was disqualified from a fourth-place finish for signing an incorrect scorecard. A journalist, Michael Bamberger, reported a day after Wie had completed her round that she had illegally dropped the ball closer to the hole than its original lie. The year 2006 involved several competitions against male competitors, and Wie finished the season with several disappointing performances in both male and female tournaments, including the Omega European Masters, the PGA 84 Lumber Classic, the LPGA Tour Samsung World Championship, and the Casio World Open. At this point, Wie had played fourteen consecutive rounds of tournament golf without breaking par, had missed the cut in eleven out of twelve tries against men, and remained winless against the women.

In 2007, Wie's slump continued, including a four-month hiatus due to injuries to both wrists, a disqualification, and several missed cuts and withdrawals. At the LPGA Ginn Tribute hosted by Annika, Wie's withdrawal was controversial, owing to the LPGA Rule of 88, which states that a non-LPGA member shooting a score of 88 or more is forced to withdraw and banned from LPGA cosponsored events for the rest of the year. Throughout the spring of 2007, Wie suffered a number of injuries and played under a great deal of pain, taking four to five painkillers a day. Notwithstanding the controversy and numerous losses, disqualifications, and injuries, Wie continuously manages to turn things to her advantage. It was written in a 2018 article that "Michelle Wie keeps putting herself back together again." Broken down by injury or illness or slump so many times in her career, she keeps finding ways to overcome. She did it again, coming from five shots behind in the final round to win the HSBC Women's World Championship in Singapore with a dramatic putt at the final hole: a thirty-six-foot birdie from just off the front of the green. Four long, frustrating years after winning the US Women's Open, Wie was finally able to claim her fifth LPGA title. Later that year, after finishing one stroke off the lead during the second round of the State Farm Classic, she was disqualified for walking outside of the official tournament area before returning to sign her scorecard. Despite the lack of victories, Wie was ranked number four in the 2007 Forbes Top 20 Earners Under 25, with annual earnings of $19 million. Wie finally became eligible to play full-time on the LPGA Tour in 2009 when she tied for seventh place at the LPGA qualifying tournament in Daytona Beach. After passing LPGA Qualifying School in December 2008, Wie declared that she still planned to play in tournaments against men. During this tournament, she also scored her first recorded hole in one as a professional.

Wie was chosen as captain for the 2009 Solheim Cup even though she was having an off year, and Wie admitted, "I cried so hard my contacts popped out...True story." Then she rewarded Coach Mallon's faith in her by going 3–0–1 in her matches and leading the team to victory. Wie was one of the few bright spots on the 2013 team that got trounced too. And more respect accrued. But Wie had no way of knowing so much friction lay ahead. Despite the publicity her appearances garnered, Wie made only one cut in a men's tournament: at the rain-shortened 2006 SK Telecom Open on the Asian Tour. She made no cuts on the PGA Tour. Wie's last appearance in a men's professional event was at the 2008 Legends Reno-Tahoe Open—an alternate event on the PGA Tour, missing the cut by nine strokes. She created controversy when, after finishing tied for twenty-sixth at the 2006 British Open, her caddie Greg Johnston was fired over the phone by Wie's then agent Ross Berlin. Johnston said he was "surprised and disappointed" at the firing and at the fact that "no one named Wie gave me the news." Wie then began working with Duncan French, who has continued caddying for her exclusively since. Wie said, "It's been a tough journey since 2014... I've had some injuries, had a really bad year, just lost a lot of confidence," and said that she is "really proud of myself for pulling myself out of it."

Wie overcame so much, winning that US Women's Open at Pinehurst in 2014, when she finally looked ready to realize all her potential in a run to number one. But she was derailed by a finger injury later that summer and then by hip, knee, and ankle injuries that led to an awful slump after that. When she finally looked as if she was turning a corner again, neck spasms and an emergency appendectomy derailed her. On Wie's physical condition, longtime swing coach David Leadbetter said, "I can't list all the injuries Michelle has had in her career... I don't think there is one joint or bone in her body that hasn't had some sort of injury or issue." In 2019, Wie West could not have imagined herself here. Chronic wrist injuries precipitated a two-year layoff that she presumed would become permanent when she became pregnant a few months after her 2019 wedding to Jonnie West, the director of basketball operations for the NBA's Golden State Warriors. She even told her husband that she was done playing. "I thought there was no chance of coming back," said Wie West. She had opportunities to move into the broadcasting booth, and motherhood seemed like a natural pivot point. "But my husband was like, 'No, no, just think it through,'" she said.

The turning point for Wie was when she learned that she was having a daughter; her feelings about a comeback shifted for reasons she struggled to articulate. And then in February, a month before her official return, Rudolph W. Giuliani, the former mayor of New York City, appeared on Steve Bannon's *War Room* podcast and asked if he could share a "funny story" about Rush Limbaugh, who had recently died. Giuliani recalled how Limbaugh had been perturbed by the photographers trailing them in a 2014 Pro-Am in which they were grouped with Wie West. Giuliani said that the "gorgeous" Wie West's putting stance was attracting the photographers, who, he said, "were trying to take pictures of her panties." Giuliani's comments crystallized Wie West's reasons for a comeback, irking her into action. After twenty-five years of speaking into a microphone as a matter of duty,

Wie West realized that she actually had a lot to say, and a return to competition would give her the platform to address inequities and ignorance that she hadn't been aware of as a teenage phenom.

More affirmation came this week as she watched Naomi Osaka, another young non-White woman who is a star in a White-majority sport, quit the French Open rather than participate in news conferences she said were damaging to her mental health. "I thought what Naomi did this past week was incredibly brave," said Wie West, who described her own experience with anxiety: "It's tough, especially when you're not doing well or there's a lot more to life than your game. There could be other stuff happening. It is sometimes crippling at times, but I'm really proud of athletes taking charge of their mental health and making it a priority. More conversations need to be had about that." Wie West is willing to wade into difficult conversations because she wants her daughter, Makenna Kamalei Yoona West, who will celebrate her first birthday on June 19, to grow up in a world where women athletes are seen and heard and enjoy equal billing with men. "I'm pretty honored that people chose to care about me," Wie West said, "but it definitely was tough at times because I went through a lot of lows, really never a moment where I could just go under the radar." A grown-up Wie West knows how to turn her anger into agency.

Currently, Wie continues to overcome a number of illnesses and injuries that have dogged her during the course of her career. She's had a bad case of strep throat that left her with a temperature of 103 in the Bahamas, an upper-respiratory infection she picked up after soldiering on to Asia, an injured ankle coddled in a Velcro brace, and four MRIs to diagnose what turned out to be bursitis in her left hip, not a tear as feared. But the hip still forced her to withdraw from some tournaments and undergo a major overhaul of her stance and her swing to be kinder to her body and reduce the enormous torque she swings and finishes with. Yet through all of the fits and starts—perhaps even because of them—most fans love Wie, and they love her big game. The LPGA commissioner Mike Whan said, "She's still one of the faces of our game. She still draws the biggest galleries here in the US and literally around the world."

J. K. Rowling, writer

Quite possibly one of the most famous and renowned former failures of our time, J. K. Rowling is the author of the wildly popular *Harry Potter* series of books. Born in 1965, she grew up with a tumultuous childhood that included a difficult and oftentimes strained relationship with her father and dealing with the illness of her mother. In 1982, at the age of seventeen years old, she attempted to gain acceptance to Oxford University. She failed and was rejected, instead enrolling at the University of Exeter, where she received her bachelor of arts in French and classics. After graduating from university, at the age of twenty-one years old, she moved to London to work for Amnesty International in 1986. After moving to Manchester with her boyfriend in 1990, at the age of twenty-five years old, while on a four-hour delayed train, the idea of a young wizard popped into Rowling's mind, later stating that it came "fully formed" and that all she needed to do was flesh out the details. Rowling would recall, "I didn't have a pen and was too shy to ask anyone for one on the train," which frustrated her at the time, but when she looks back, it was the best thing for her. It gave her the full four hours on the train to think up all the ideas for the book. As the narrative unfolded, Rowling had a dream. The dream was to share this story with readers, both young and old. With steely determination, Rowling spent hours in nearby cafés, enthusiastically plotting her story—her daughter in her pram nearby.

However, it was just a few short months after that, that her mother, Anne, died from multiple sclerosis, leaving her extremely distraught and upset. In the wake of her mother's death, only a few months afterward, she moved to Porto, in Portugal, to teach English. There, she met a man, got married, got pregnant, and gave birth to her daughter, who was born in 1993. The relationship was a very strenuous one, with reports of domestic abuse resulting in a separation and eventual divorce. With only three chapters of *Harry Potter* completed at the end of 1993, when she was at the age of thirty-eight years old, she moved to Edinburgh to live with her sister. "I was jobless, a lone parent, and as poor as it is possible to be in modern Britain without being homeless," she said in her commencement speech at Harvard. During this period, her depression took a dark turn, and she considered herself a failure. She had fallen and felt stuck. She even contemplated suicide.

At that point, she considered herself a major failure. She had failed at just about everything she had ever attempted to do in life. She was diagnosed with clinical depression and was suicidal. Luckily, she found it in her to seek help, and writing became an outlet. The whole world now knows the story of the boy who lived, but not many people know the struggle behind his creation. It holds a very practical lesson. Two years later, in 1995, five years after the initial idea had come to her, she managed to finish the manuscript for *Harry Potter and the Sorcerer's Stone*. She located an agent, but after one year of trying to get it published, all twelve major publishing houses had rejected her book. Seemingly definitive failures can often be debilitating. They break many, but J. K. Rowling's story provides a rich narrative for how this kind of failure can be made temporary with the right approach. With the onset of her depression and the lack of visible opportunity, Rowling treated her rock bottom as a conclusion, and the feeling that accompanied her failure was acceptance. She believed in the story she told herself. That began to change after her visit to seek help. With time, she realized that though her situation was what it was, it could also be more. With defeat behind her, she was left with great upside potential and little downside risk.

When Rowling returned to the UK without a job, she produced far more in the next few years than she had in the years leading up to her new life. She attributes this to the routine guided by the simplicity of her life. There wasn't much she could do, so she would pretty much just get up in the morning and go to a café. Her daughter would sleep, and she would write. Such limitations also drive resourcefulness. When we have more, we follow existing patterns built into our environment. We have less of an incentive to look beyond what's immediately accessible and how it's presented. That isn't the case with less. If you want to keep moving, you have to think outside the box. You're pushed to be creative, and that sparks inspiration. Failure often simplifies, and it eliminates. It removes any excess noise, and though these limitations may initially appear as hurdles, if you use them right, they actually free you to better stimulate momentum. The likelihood of success depends on the effectiveness of output and the consistency of effort. It's not only about creating great work, but it's also about how far you're willing to go for it. Rowling is now a globally renowned author. Her success with the *Harry Potter* series can't just be attributed to luck. Critics widely agree that she's a talented writer, and the rest of us can attest to the beauty of her imagination. In spite of that, she didn't always have the easiest time convincing others of that.

Today, the first book alone has sold more than 100 million copies, and the combined series is estimated to have sold close to 400 million. It's the highest-selling book series in the world. In hindsight, it's easy to laugh at the absurdity of it all. But what if she had quit after that first round of rejections? It's almost a scary thought, but it's not an unreasonable one. Now, this isn't to say that we should always push ahead in spite of external circumstances, such as discussed above. Sometimes we're just not good enough, and sometimes the reward is insignificant relative to the risk. It's important to have checks and balances in place to provide a sanity check. The only real point is that persistence matters. Rejection and failure may not be easy to absorb, but if you have a rational reason to believe that what you have to offer is of value, then showing up and trying again and again is a critical part of any strategy for success. In statistics, the law of large numbers dictates that if our sample size is small, then factors of chance play a greater role in determining an outcome. For example, if you flip a coin twice, you could very well land on tails with each flip even though the probability of each avenue is even. If you flip a coin two hundred times, however, you're far less likely to have randomly skewed results.

There are two kinds of failure: temporary failures, which occur throughout any process and help drive progress, and definitive failures, which occur less frequently but can change how we see ourselves. They can be debilitating. J. K. Rowling has been there. Before her status as the most successful living author, she had her own struggles. Mentally, these struggles weren't too different from the kind that the rest of us face from time to time. Rowling finished the first two books while still on welfare benefits. The Dementors introduced in the third book were inspired by her mental illness. It wasn't until 1996 when a small literary house in London named Bloomsbury gave the green light and a very small advance of £1,500 only due to the behest of the owner's daughter that the book was published. In 1997, seven years after the initial idea for the young wizard, the first *Harry Potter* book was published. By 2004, Rowling had become the first author to become a billionaire through book writing, according to Forbes.

Pierre N. McDonnaugh, me

Yes, me! You may be wondering how I got to sit in the company of the greats like Rowling, Jobs, Jordan, and others mentioned above. Although I don't have the stature and great success they have had, I do share the ups and downs that they've had and the failures they've had with all the despair and frustration that comes with it, and so have you! Recall the point here: this was a story about failure and how we can all learn from it—not just through the transparent experiences of the rich and famous but from my and your experiences with failure! This is what you and I have in common with those that have crossed the proverbial finish line in life. The only difference is that we are still striving. That's all, so don't sell yourself short because we still have much to learn. Now back to my story...

Some time ago, I travelled to Las Vegas to visit my ailing mother, who was struggling with cancer. I realized at that time that this would most likely be the last time I would have this opportunity. Sitting at the foot of my mother's deathbed, I thought back on the "ashes" and could not help thinking about my personal run-ins with failure throughout the duration of my life and the ashes upon which I stand. When I consider my relationship with failure, I credit my parents. As I mentioned earlier, one's tolerance toward risk is embedded in one's culture and in one's parents as to how that may or may not be expressed as a result. When it comes to assumption of risk, people from the Caribbean maintain a more relaxed attitude in which practice counts more than principles and deviance from the norm is more easily tolerated. Hofstede observes this about people from the Caribbean in his cultural scales, where people from the Caribbean are considered low-uncertainty-avoidance (UAI) societies. The UAI dimension has to do with the way that a society deals with the fact that the future can never be known: should we try to control the future or just let it happen? This ambiguity brings with it anxiety, and different cultures have learned to deal with this anxiety in different ways. The extent to which the members of a culture feel threatened by ambiguous or unknown situations and have created beliefs and institutions that try to avoid these is reflected in the score on uncertainty avoidance. Low-scoring countries on this dimension have a low preference for avoiding uncertainty, or its members have higher risk tolerance than most. In fact, societies exhibiting low UAI believe there should be no more rules than are necessary, and if they are ambiguous or do not work, they should be abandoned or changed. Schedules are flexible, hard work is undertaken when necessary but not for its own sake, precision and punctuality do not come naturally, and innovation is not seen as threatening. As an illustration of how this plays out, just think of the Olympic Jamaican bobsled team, the Trinidadian steel pan made out of discarded oil drums, Usain Bolt and the Jamaican track-and-field dynasty, reggae and reggaeton, the rum industry, Dominican baseball, or just about anything that came out of Cuba in the last seventy years, and the list goes on. This is a culture where if they don't have it, they make it up! I am proud to say this runs through my blood as well.

I was born in Bradford-upon-Avon, England, by Caribbean par-

ents in a place called Woolley
Grange, outside the town of
Bath. It's a very nice country
manor estate. More like a castle,
I might add, which at the time

was donated to England's National Health Service (NHS) to provide as

a dormitory for its nursing students who came over from the Caribbean

during the Windrush after WWII. I was unaware of this period in

English history and its significance to modern England until I moved to

London much later life. When the *Empire Windrush* passenger ship

docked at Tilbury, England, from Jamaica on June 22, 1948, it marked

the start of the postwar immi-
gration boom, which was to
change British society. Images
of the African-Caribbean
passengers filing off the gang-

plank have become part of the country's social history. After WWII,

Britain encouraged immigration from Commonwealth countries. To a

large extent, this was to help rebuild the country as there was a shortage

of labor at the time. The *Empire Windrush* carried 492 migrants who were coming to a country promising prosperity and employment in exchange for their service. These migrants and their descendants are referred to as the Windrush generation. Among them were the calypso artists "Lord Kitchener" and "Lord Beginner" and onboard the many ships that would follow in this mass migration would ultimately be my father Lionel McDonnaugh from Jamaica. A bit later came my mother, Barbara Reece, from Trinidad. Arrivals were temporarily housed near Brixton; the town's Windrush Square commemorates the ship's arrival (British Library). The majority remained to settle permanently and now form a central part of British society. This is where my parents met, married, had my brothers—Andre and Shaun—and me. We subsequently migrated to New York after my mother was recruited as a registered nurse/midwife at Gouverneur Health (formerly Gouverneur Hospital), which was a municipally owned healthcare facility in New York City affiliated with the New York University School of Medicine. We moved to East Elmhurst Queens, where they bought a home that would be in our family until my father retired many years later.

Lionel, my father, had worked many jobs. Although a trained diesel mechanic, he could fix just about anything. He was a very stable guy and worked only two jobs in his entire life, each for almost twenty years: at Brinks Armored Trucks and the New York Metropolitan

Transit Authority. If you are thinking, *Wait, but they don't have trucks,* you would be right. Near the latter half of his working years, he moved to an inside job and retrained to become refrigeration mechanic until retirement. Dad was very industrious and creative, as were most of his baby-boomer peers, and he had many side hustles. Chief among them, he owned a number of residential properties around greater New York City—everything from small multifamily dwellings and single homes to a thirty-two-unit apartment building on Rutland Road in Brooklyn to a gas station that he owned with his good friend Cox (or at least "good friend" until they unwound the gas station). He also ran an auto repair service from the backyard on the weekends for the neighbor's car care needs. Dad told me that before coming to America, he owned an apartment building near Brixton to house primarily newly arriving friends and family coming over from Jamaica. During that time, he found it difficult to source indigenous food types and quality that he was used to back home. He said he would drive out to the country on the weekends and buy fresh meats and vegetables because in Jamaica, they mostly ate chicken, goat, and pork but not much beef as it was expensive; and the chicken was mostly fresh whereas in London, it was not. A neighbor from the building, upon seeing his groceries, asked how he came to have fresh groceries. He told the story, and they asked if he could shop for them on his next run, to which he replied yes. Not long after word got out, Dad ended up shopping for the building and building a small shed to carve up the meat for delivery to the residents. He told me that on one particular run, he saw the farmer had a goat. He asked, "How much for the goat?" The farmer asked why, as the English did not customarily eat goats but kept them as pets. Realizing how much he could get for the parts, Dad told the man he wanted a pet 'round the house. Dad paid for the goat and was off—to the shed where he carved up the goat and sold it to his neighbors. He said he never made so much money in one go!

My mother was officially a registered nurse/midwife, but when not working for a hospital, she was largely in practice for herself. For a time in the 1970s, Mom was the midwife to Long Island's rich and famous as she ran up and down the North Shore in the middle of the night, delivering the babies of many of Long Island's wealthiest residents. I think that having a midwife in those days was a bit of a status symbol as it was very uncommon in the US; it was more of a British thing. Mom had her share of side hustles too as she was part of a Windrush mafia: a group of Caribbean nurses who, after saving England's NHS, also left the UK in search of economic opportunities of the new world. These women of differing specializations would maintain an underground network of who was paying what rate and for what nursing services, and they would trade off the opportunities they could not staff to each other. This covered everything from home births to private duty care for elderly and special needs to hospital jobs and beyond. They even had an underground banking infrastructure, the susu,[1] which we won't get into at this time. This was how they survived and thrived.

Needless to say, the love affair did not last long at all, which any casual observer could have seen coming a mile away. My dad was really old school—a conservative Jamaican, and Mom, Trinidadian, always wanting to make a big splash, be seen in the right places, and take in all the new world had to offer: cars, fashion, big city, bright lights, and all that crap. Jamaicans are all about work and money, and Trinidadians are all about "Where's the party at?"…not typically a match made in heaven. They were doomed from the start. In fact, we set foot in America in 1965, and they split up in 1970, when I was five. With my mother deciding to move out, we moved to a very small two-bedroom apartment on Northern Boulevard in Jackson

---

[1]   A sou-sou (also spelled sou sou, su-su, or susu) is an informal rotating savings club where a group of people get together and contribute an equal amount of money into a fund weekly, bi-weekly, or monthly. The total pool, also known as a hand, is then paid to one member of the club on a previously agreed-on schedule.

Heights, Queens, above a Carvel ice-cream shop. My brothers and I, however partially poor at the time, still attended private school thanks to my dad, which was a bit of a weird mix—poor kids in private school. I recall playing on the roof of the ice-cream shop and throwing things down at walk-up patrons looking for ice cream in the heat of the New York summer. We lived there with my uncle Hollis, Mom's older brother; in fact, we lived most places with Hollis. He and his problems were a regular presence in our lives, but he was Mom's older brother after all. He was family, as my mom would say.

One year on New Year's Eve, shortly after he moved his girl-friend in with us, who I believe he met in Germany, they were all planning to go out without her. They argued all evening, and after he left to party without her, she cried, or should I say bawled, all evening while my brother and I tried to drown it out, locked up in our room, playing "Six Gun Shooting Gallery" and waiting for the ball to drop at Times Square on the television. I think this is why I hate crying so much to this day. Those were very cold winters back then; I recall eating breakfast cereal with hot milk and Mom heating my pants on the oven door each morning before school, even burning them on one occasion, which is a bit weird to explain. We frequently used the oven to supplement the heat. But hard times would soon be over as Mom found a surrogate buyer to secure a single-family home in Hempstead, Long Island—the suburbs.

Maybe I should explain. In 1970, America was in the midst of desegregation and forced integration as an offshoot of the civil rights movements in the preceding years. This culminated in practices such as redlining, mortgage discrimination, and racially restrictive covenants in housing. Redlining is the systematic denial of various services by federal government agencies, local governments, as well as the private sector either directly or through the selective raising of prices (Gross, T. 2019). This meant that frequently, when minority applicants went seeking housing in certain areas, they could not go where they wanted unless they had some tricks up their sleeve. My mother had a friend (a White friend) feign interest in the property she wanted (a straw purchaser) and subsequently secure the property, only to show up at the last minute as the true purchaser, which, of course, at that point is too late to withdraw the property from consideration without appearing blatantly racist by all, not to mention illegal. Hence, we were moving to Hempstead! It was 1970, and I was going to first grade and my new life in America.

As kids, in our first year in the new house, we would walk the neighborhood, selling old magazines door-to-door, but for the most part, we just played around the house. We didn't know anyone at the time, so my mother encouraged us to go to the Percy Jackson Youth Center in Hempstead. We walked there only to find what appeared to be a pool hall for kids. This was well before video games, but the next best thing was bumper pool. We hung out there for a bit until it got weird when some local kids saw we were outsiders. We took the hint and never went back.

Hempstead was as rough place then, as rough as it is now. When we first arrived in Long Island, as the youngest of three, I often felt overlooked and disregarded. I was a latchkey kid for as long as I could remember, which was a term coined by middle-class Whites for letting yourself in the house each day because no one was typically home—single-parent household. In the ensuing years, I would experience scores of failures, more than I care to count, of all stripes and colors and most certainly more than most of my peers. I never fit in as an immigrant—a Black one at that—among Long Island's mix of Irish and Italian kids. By comparison, I dressed funny, talked funny, and ate weird-smelling food, among other things. I was determined, however, to make it work. I attended Grand Avenue School, just over the bridge from our new house in a neighboring town called Baldwin. Although we lived in Hempstead, it was along a border of the Hempstead and Uniondale school districts; referred to as "the other side." Each day, I and a small cadre of other (mostly Black) kids would walk a short way down Baldwin Road, over the bridge to school. We all grew to know each other and become friends, if for no other reason than the daily walk together. Grand Avenue was a mostly White school in an all-White part of town, and it always seemed strange to me that we went there even though there were many schools just as close on the Hempstead side of town. It seemed strange to me because it was as hostile as it was nice and familiar. Although we were very unwelcomed on that side of the bridge, I had all White friends through junior high school. These were kids I remember to this day who I loved and enjoyed, but beyond that, I feared for my life when moving within their community alone.

My first-grade teacher Mrs. Blunt, she was mean, intolerant, and impatient (and to be honest, probably racist); but as a kid, you were not sensitive to what motivated such behaviors. There were no more than a couple of Black kids in each class, and from day one, she sat me at the back of the room, which would not be the first time. I recall a time where I was punished with detention for struggling to properly write the letter *P*, and my brother, who walked us home each day, had to wait in the back of the room for me and my punishment. He had asthma and every now and then would have labored breathing. As he sat, waiting for me and breathing hard, Mrs. Butler yelled at him, "If you insist on breathing like that, you can wait outside!" He got up and left. Ultimately, my mother was called in because while she was shouting at me about my abhorrent writing style, she said my *P*s looked like lollipops and were trash fit for the garbage. And she threw the paper back at me. Understanding they were fit for the trash, I picked up the paper then threw it in the trash. She didn't like that and thought I was being a smart-ass. My mother thought it was the funniest thing.

During my first month in class, a kid next door who also apparently was a problem was removed and sent to our class while they went out to recess. Let's just call him Eric in respect of his privacy. He was seated next to me, and I was scared of the kid labeled as bad (believing to myself I was one of the good ones). He whispered to a me, "Hey." I refused to make eye contact, and he whispered again and introduced himself. He said his name was Eric. He became one of my oldest and best friends. Eric was Black like me and a rough kid from a big family, and he didn't give a shit! Eric's family moved to Long Island sometime earlier than we did from Brooklyn. His teacher, Ms. Fontana, made Mrs. Butler look like Mother Teresa! She would hit kids on their heads with pencils and regularly chastise and, yes, was also probably racist. Eric was everything I wasn't, and I was lucky to have him as a friend at that time in my life.

Things revolved around Eric. Each day, he made the walk to school an adventure; he did perfect cartwheels and backflips, would terrorize White kids, would make the girls run and scream with his threats, and left most adults and school staff horrified with his antics. Most of all, Eric made me feel safe because I was his friend, and everyone else was afraid. My time spent with Eric was often the most exciting and the most horrific at the same time. He would rock climb the side of the trestle across the Southern State Parkway at Exit 21, which, at the time, had no fence like it does today—most likely thanks to Eric. We would play tag in homes under construction and chase pigeons in abandoned grain silos that he enthusiastically called pigeon towers. When we needed money, we would follow Eric to the supermarket to bag groceries at the end of the bagging lane and carry bags to the car for tips. Eric's early recollection of me was a weird kid with "hard shoes," running and sliding in the halls. American kids didn't wear shoes, as my mother insisted. Needless to say, adults like Mrs. Butler and Ms. Fontana were my introduction to failure as a self-image, but I didn't care because I had my friends. This was the first time, as a five-year-old, to be viewed as a failure on sight before I opened my mouth; to be viewed by an adult with contempt as if you alone were the problem was a very powerful and insidious force of nature at such an early age. Adults such as these destroyed the lives of many Black and brown children of the time.

I used to refer to our house as the Kool-Aid house (after a popular TV commercial at the time) because it was where most neighborhood kids hung out since Mom regularly worked till late. Our friends were a bit crazy, though, and ran the spectrum from gangsters and criminals to the kindest and most caring people. This is where I realized that you shouldn't judge people by their circumstances because we are born into them; people are much bigger than what they do or the mistakes they make. I recall summers hanging out on Botsford Street, at the side of our house, playing football in the street (or more like watching as I was too young to play). I would get my hair braided and unbraided every weekend by the older girls. They would have massive water balloon fights and stay up late in the evening, talking. Those days were amazing; it was a time of Black pride, dashikis, afros, blowouts, marshmallow shoes, leisure suits, *Soul Train* Saturdays, bicycle tag, and trips to the deli for bags of candy and garlic pickles. All in all, I enjoyed it all. Taking the good with the bad life in Hempstead was amazing, and I wouldn't change a thing.

The primary school years for me (1971–1976) were very happy and very lonely. I enjoyed the company of my brothers. Andre, my older brother, was "the man"; he immediately made many friends that regularly hung around the house. Back in the '70s, he got DJ equipment and started a crew called the Daily News back when it wasn't even popular to do so. He was also a local streetball legend on the basketball court. Andre's crew was very popular, so much so that everywhere I went, my name was Andre's Brother. Other than that, no one knew who I was. His notoriety trickled down to Shaun and me as well such that we came up in the shadow of his street credibility. Back in those days, "having back" was critically important in places like Hempstead. *Back* meant a bunch of people who go to bat for you no matter what; today, it's what you would call a "ride or die" friend and family network. As the youngest of three charismatic brothers, negotiating the streets was easy—because you didn't have to. Notwithstanding all of that, none of it mattered on the White side of the bridge. That was a different story.

Shaun and I got into many adventures together like a modern-day urban Huckleberry Finn. We were very conservative and like-minded as kids go. Shaun was nothing short of amazing. He was a straight *A* student in school while everyone respected him on the street. He was always sharply dressed and had a characteristic low haircut—almost bald. Everything he touched, he studied first, whether it was martial arts, raising and training dogs, or making music. Also, he played the trumpet so well he had a solo at the ninth-grade band concert in front of the entire school. He excelled in sports, particularly in the track and field relay, being the fastest on the team, as well as football and basketball. Oh, and let's not forget French studies, where he achieved an award for studying the French language and culture beyond the level required of high school, resulting in an invitation to study in a summer program in Cannes, south of France. Shaun loved all things financial and studied asset management in high school while trading securities with his allowance in his Schwab One account. He ultimately won the EAB-sponsored LIBEC Businessman's Award, which was an all-Long Island accounting award that came with permanent summer employment at EAB

Bank (now part of Citigroup). It was a competition among all high schools, public and private, in New York.

We were only one year apart in age, and I was fortunate enough to grow up in his shadow...not. In fact, I recall at his award ceremony, after he won about five different awards, the event coordinator (and my then English teacher), Ms. Leadbetter, one of the only African American teachers at the school, could not wait to greet our parents as she was so excited to express how proud of him she was. I was sitting in the auditorium with my parents at the end of the ceremony, waiting for Shaun to come over. Ms. Leadbetter came over and reached us about the same time as Shaun (with all of his awards) and went on to share her excitement at how proud she was and how amazing she thought he was. As I stood in the back of the group, towering over them, as I am pretty tall, we locked eyes; and her demeanor quickly changed as she bristled and became agitated. Losing focus on the accolades, Ms. Leadbetter abruptly said to me, "What, what can I do for you?" Puzzled, I said, "I am with them." She could not have been more shocked, stating, "Are you two from the same family?" My dad looked over at me in disgust while nervous laughter emanated from everyone else; I was used to that at this point, however. Nothing will make you feel more like a loser than growing up in the shadow of a superstar brother.

Shaun on the street was no different. He and his crew, Glass Gardens, were the leading local DJs in Hempstead at the time and would regularly battle other crews for local dominance at house parties, halls, block parties, etc. Who said being smart wasn't cool? The thing about Shaun is he was not just a DJ, but he had back (muscle), weapons, and no shortage of party favors to keep things interesting. While I used the allowance our dad gave us to buy junk food, candy, and comics, Shaun re-upped with weed (*marijuana*) and used the profits to buy clothes (as a teen, he was always dressed for Wall Street) and the latest DJ equipment: Numark mixers, echo chambers, microphones, diamond tipped needles, Cerwin Vega bass bottom speakers (to stack), etc. He would then invest his earnings in stocks

and bonds. Always enterprising, always making money, Shaun was only one year older, but it may as well have been  twenty—looking like a business man at sixteen. While Shaun took after my father with his financial acuity, I, on the other hand, took after my mother: no matter how much she made delivering babies, she never had enough. I had much to learn.

Oh, you may be wondering why I had not continued the DJ dynasty, the legacy. Well, as you might imagine, at this point in the story, I did, but not so successfully. When my time came, I inherited Andre's old equipment while he was away in college. I hooked up with a buddy of mine and started a small crew. Our first party was the birthday party of a neighbor. She would pay $100 for the night. The party started off as good as can be imagined. It was packed, and the music was booming as my partner rocked the turntables. This was before rap took hold and when people were playing Georgio Moroder; Earth, Wind, & Fire; Parliament-Funkadelic, Kraftwerk (out of Germany), and "Good Times" by Chic. Right at the end of a set of my partner scratching "Good Times," he waved me in, saying he needed a break. We just started, and the basement was a dark sweat box. With only the light above the DJ table, you could see the crowd moving and swaying to the beat. However, as soon as I put on the headphones, I could hear nothing; when I looked up, I saw him running up the stairs—with this knowledge. I yelled to him, but he was gone. I suspect the mixer was too weak to power the headphones, so you could barely hear the other turntable. I tried to switch turn-tables with the crossfader and threw the beat off because I could not hear a thing. Again and again, nothing. What I could hear, however, was boos from the crowd as people even stopped dancing. Looking at all the angry faces staring back at me, I was mortified and panicking when, just then, I saw Shaun come down the stairs. I called him over and asked, pleaded with him, to use his mixer, and he just shook his head no. He told me to give up the money and that he would finish the party. I looked over at the crying birthday girl whose party I was ruining and handed my brother the headphones. I just went home in shame and never did another party. My brother, you gotta love him. What made me such a quitter, I will never know, but I had no confidence in myself, no patience, no courage to blow things up, no emotional strength, and, as a result, no persistence to stick out the bad times and no success. In hindsight, this was nobody's fault but my own; it's what I had become.

These were also very lonely years for me because I never quite fit in socially, was frequently alone, and now anxious about my academic failings in junior high school. All I had was sports. I recall a meeting my mother had with my ninth-grade guidance counselor, who wanted to hold me back for failing too many subjects. She was pleading with the woman to allow me to move on to high school and promising that I would make up the difference in high school. The guidance counselor bought the excuses and allowed me to advance but admonished me, "Listen, young man, life is hard, and you cannot just get through on good looks and a smile!" Apparently, the joke was on her as I went on to a life in sales, but more on that later (all kidding aside, she was right). In high school, I did no better as I failed math every year with *F*s, and *F* means zero credit. Was I really that bad? Did I get it all wrong? No credit, not even for showing up? It was so bad that my junior-year math teacher pulled me aside and showed me my grade. He said, "You see that?" looking at a 70 inside a small circle. "That's your grade." I was confused, but seeing the 70 made me a bit happy at the same time. He then said, "What that means is I never want to see you in here again. It means you actually failed. But after four years, you must have learned something, so get out." As excited as I was to never see math again, I went on to more years of being removed from classes for being disruptive (I was very funny, or so my friends thought), being listed as ineligible for sports, and just generally blowing it.

My insecurities, bad habits, and lack of confidence only continued in high school as poor academic performance continued largely because I was intellectually immature in that I didn't understand the gravity or significance or even the importance of studying, working hard, and getting good grades. The good news, however, was that I was getting much better in basketball—'cause that's where all my time went, unfortunately. Maybe it was escapism, but all I wanted to do was play basketball at the expense of all else. Notwithstanding racking up the failures, I was a naturally inquisitive boy, actually enjoyed high school, and was having a really good time. However, for whatever reason, school just failed to hold my attention. I was disruptive, frequently got in trouble, and was regularly removed from class. This was a pattern for me until I got to twelfth grade. However, I didn't care because I was certain that basketball would be my savior and make it all

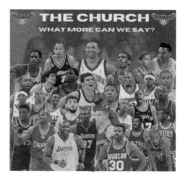

right. The only thing was that in order to play sports, a *C* average must be maintained, and I did not. So I was ineligible and could not play

for my high school in my final year, which was detrimental to any possibility of continuing on a college team. Luckily, in 1981, I had the opportunity to play for Ernie Lorch's

Riverside Church Hawks. This was the best of all possible outcomes given the circumstances, and I made one of New York's most prestigious AAU basketball programs in Harlem that year. I was fortunate enough during the summer of my eleventh-grade year to be introduced to Coach Lorch by John Salley while at Five-Star Basketball Camp in Bryn Mawr, Pennsylvania. Everyone who was anyone in New York basketball passed through Riverside at one point (and Five-Star Basketball Camp, for that matter). Lorch, a multimillionaire corporate attorney, turned Riverside Church into an elite program before allegations of sexual abuse of a former player led to his resignation in 2002. According to *New York Post*'s Zach Brazilier, Lorch's best team featured Metta World Peace, Elton Brand, Erick Barkley, Andrew Glover, and Lamar Odom, which lost one game all summer. Others to pass through the program included Mark Jackson, Walter Berry, Chris Mullin, Malik Sealy, Kenny Smith, and Albert King. "Ernie Lorch, at one time, was probably the most powerful man in the high school/AAU basketball community on the East Coast," Konchalski said. "Riverside Church was the gold standard of AAU programs." Lorch ran Riverside Church from 1961 to 2002 and began the athletic program, which included baseball and football, as an outreach for troubled teenagers. I was back in play, and the dream was still alive! All I needed to do was graduate high school. However, in keeping with my cognitive dissonance, as my basketball prospects soared, my grades had completely fallen off. As my final year progressed, my high school coach was receiving college letters of interest in me almost weekly for schools that either saw me in camp that last summer or in Riverside games. I was flying high until the realization that I would not be graduating at the end of the year. When I failed to graduate, everything took a slow turn for the worst.

Wondering why I no longer heard from the schools that were interested in me, I reached out to the coach at Columbia University, who showed an early interest in me joining their program, to ask what happened. He put it bluntly that I would not work out as a student athlete in their program and that I was no longer under consideration. This, too, was the case for Farleigh Dickenson, Dowling College, and others. I was devastated as the realization set in that because I didn't graduate, all these letters of interest dried up, and I was no longer being contacted by anyone. I fell into depression that summer as I went to summer school to try to complete my final year. I wouldn't walk with the rest of my class, but at least I would be able to move on to college the following year, which was my intention. I understood Coach Lorch to be a resource for kids like me as I heard so much about how he had a reputation for looking out for his players. It was said that on occasion, he paid the tuition of several Catholic school players across the city. He would purchase dress clothes for players and arrange for travel so they could get home at a reasonable hour in addition to bankrolling the month-long trips over the summer for a number of his teams. He arranged for them to attend individual showcases and was there for kids in need. In fact, it was well known, according to Cardozo coach Ron Naclerio, that when "kids got arrested or had a legal problem, they called 1-800-Ernie Lorch. He was the first guy there to bail them out." It was truly an unusual thing to see this middle-aged White guy, a midtown millionaire attorney, making a regular appearance at the Rucker Park in Harlem to watch the summer league games and be welcomed by the community as everyone knew exactly who he was.

Luckily, I would experience Coach Lorch's kindness and generosity firsthand when he empathized with my predicament. After our season ended, he enrolled me in a tournament called Athletes for Better Education that summer. This tournament was an opportunity open to college basketball programs to get a last look at anyone they may have overlooked in the recruiting process, among other things. It was a five-day team tournament with over two hundred coaches a day watching games all day each day. I did very well and was picked up by the Fashion Institute of Technology. Technically, it was a four-year program, but they played NJCAA sports. And most importantly, they were ranked fifth and seventh, respectively, in the two years I was in attendance.

If I wanted a second chance at basketball, this was it, and I was ready—or so I thought. On the first year at FIT, although I was a success in basketball, I continued failing and struggling in academics. By the middle of the second year, the season was nearing an end. FIT was number one in New York State for the two years running, and we were about to go to the playoffs in Kansas for the NJCAA national championships. After we won our game and secured state championship status, the college president came to the locker room to congratulate us personally and let us know our season was officially over! His stated reason was that, of the eleven of us, seven had less than a 2.0 GPA, myself among them. Standing there, half-dressed at my locker, I had to reevaluate my future. In particular, my GPA was a 1.0 and probably the worst of the bunch. I'd spent two years in junior college and aspired to an *F*. It was time to back away from school and rethink my plans, which, in hindsight, was a very good thing given the amount of top-performing basketball players that ended up nowhere.

It's amazing to consider the wasted talents of these kids who sacrificed it all for the game, even in football and baseball, for that matter, and make it big, only to be worse off in the end, whereas if they aspired to normal aspirations like plumbers, police, doctors, lawyers etc., at least they would have jobs well into retirement. Many former professional athletes end up broke and penniless. You work so hard to end up nowhere. I guess I dodged a bullet on that one.

Needless to say, I left school altogether at this point as I was just making a mess of things. I dropped out and took a job at the law firm, Hayt, Hayt, & Landau, in Great Neck, Long Island, retrieving medical records from New York-area hospitals. I drove a company car and wore a suit at nineteen years old. It was an amazing job and an amazing opportunity for someone who just dropped out of college

and didn't have any other education to speak of. However, I somehow seemed to mess that up as well. I took frequent advances against my paycheck and ran up an overdraft account on my first-ever bank account. During the occasional workday, when I was supposed to be pulling medical records, I was playing basketball at the park with my friends in a suit and tie. I decided to leave the job and found myself sleeping most days and roaming the streets of NYC most nights as my friends were either at school or working. These were the streets of 1980s NYC; it's other-worldly by today's standards. In fact, the only people out at night were the police and criminals. It was like watching TV except it was live. Eventually, this life terrified me, and I knew I had to get out of there before I played a leading role in the next episode.

It was then I enlisted in the USAF. The military never looked better as I told no one and never looked back. I didn't even tell my mother, which, needless to say, didn't go over very well. Once I arrived at my permanent location at Travis AFB, I realized that having a real job, being on my own, and having a wife and kids really sobered me up for the first time ever. I enrolled in a capstone program to complete my undergraduate degree, which I attended on most weekends. I took courses at a local community college in the evenings to complete the program even faster. I started a second job, cleaning carpets on the nights I was not attending school. This was a major transition for me as I was adjusting to fatherhood and the world of work, not to mention life in the military itself. It was the most difficult time of my life as the adjustment was anything but smooth. I recall the frustration one evening after cleaning carpets until 2:00 a.m., getting home so hungry, and smelling food but seeing none. I was sad, angry, and wondering how my life ended up here. Exhausted and with everyone in the house asleep, I sat on the floor of my living room and put on a Ray Charles album. I was on the brink of tears while listening to Ray Charles, knowing this needed to change and wondering if all this was God punishing me for my earlier sins. I was twenty-three with two children, no degree, and no prospects to think of, and I was not doing well at the mental health clinic where I worked at the time either. I was discharged from the Air Force in 1988, and I had just broken up with my spouse the year earlier. I was a semester short of completing my degree and was desperate to do whatever I needed to support the family. After a year in sales as a door-to-door insurance man and selling photocopiers in strip malls, I was sleeping on a friend's floor until I passed the Series seven Registered Representative exam. It was here when things began to change. This license enabled me to sell securities, and I was officially a stockbroker.

This was 1989, and all around Wall Street, there was no shortage of penny stock firms ready and willing to rip off unsuspecting clients. I saw opportunity in this, having no pedigree to get into the big firms: I knew if I could get sponsored for the license, I could navigate my way to big-name firms. I had no problem getting an interview and knew if I could hype up the greed, I was in. It worked, and I got picked up by a penny stock firm called Stuart James. Although I had no intention of cheating clients, the plan was to blow out as soon as I got the license. My big break would come as soon as I took the exam in the role of sales assistant to Peter Camejo, the president of Progressive Asset Management, a regional broker dealer in Oakland California. Expecting very little of me as I was an admin, my new boss regularly provided me with lead cards, stating, "If you get 'em, you can keep 'em," promising to make me a producer someday. That day came a short year later when he found out that I had raised over $1 million dollars in assets off lead cards in my spare time. Keeping true to the promise, he would soon give me an opportunity to be a producer. I subsequently moved my business to Smith Barney in Berkeley, transferring my entire client book. About a year into this new role, I felt a tremendous relief that I had finally arrived. I reconciled with my wife, and things appeared to be looking up.

However, on my birthday of that year, my spouse succumbed to a lifetime of battling with depression and had commit suicide shortly after our most recent breakup (which there were three), leaving me to raise our twin sons on my own. I thought it best to move back to New York, where I could get the help of family. I had yet to complete my undergraduate degree—which was on hold for the time being—and was still struggling to manage my client book and make sales while raising two children in NYC. Being a broker was an amazing role that came with a great deal of ownership, autonomy, and accountability to your clients. Only your character and wits stood between yourself and their absolute financial ruin, and I loved the importance it bestowed upon me. The job was very rewarding as it required constantly marketing yourself at seminars and speaking engagements, holding nonprofit officer posts, and attending lots of dinners and black-tie functions. At this point, I joined a number of organizations including 100 Black Men of New York, where I met some of my closest friends. However, running back and forth with children as a single parent, I found myself faced with being a bad dad and a bad broker and had to let it all go as one of the last vestiges of my old life. I fell back on completing my education in order to move forward. I quit banking altogether and dedicated the next two years to getting into law school. Refusing to accept no for an answer, I committed to applying to every bar-accredited law school there was until one of them allowed me admittance. I enrolled in Kaplan's LSAT program, applied to five schools that first year, and got five "ding" letters (like a bell that goes *ding* each time you get rejected). The painful part is that you have to wait six months to hear that you didn't make it. Keeping true to the plan, on that second year, I repeated the Kaplan course, rewrote my essay, and applied to another five schools. After the eighth rejection letter, Detroit Mercy Law Center wait-listed me, and I would get an acceptance to Howard University School of Law! I went on to graduate from Howard University School of Law in the class of 1999, achieve an LLM from the Washington School of Law at American University in 2005, and ultimately earn a doctoral degree from the Lubin School of Business at Pace University in New York, majoring in international business management and economics.

In my life, I have seen the highest of highs and lowest of lows but appreciate every minute of the journey, failures and all. I can attribute my achievements in life to my attitude toward failure in that I felt like I failed so much that it stopped hurting me, and I was immune from its emotional effects. I was so focused on becoming a better version of myself that I failed to recognize the pain or the cost. I just knew it would only get better as the only way for me to go was up. Additionally, there were scores of amazing people who came in and out of my life at pinnacle moments along the way, like Disney side characters (e.g., Jiminy Cricket, Timon and Pumba, etc.), whose influence in my life was invaluable in making me the person I am today. A Buddhist principle teaches that when the student is ready, the teacher will appear. Maybe such people were always there, but I lacked the humility and wherewithal to recognize their value and significance to me.

Great achievement came with great sacrifice. As I have lost a great deal along the way, I gained the emotional strength and courage to appreciate the journey. I lost my first wife, and my eldest children grew up without a mother. They had to endure my difficulties and instabilities along the way. They spent many hours alone before I understood the value of my presence in their lives. My second marriage didn't go so well either. However, it was the failures that provided the insight and directionality of the changes I needed in my life to be a better version of myself. Some changes were more painful than others. I not only found the emotional strength and courage to withstand the challenges that lay before me but also the strength to bear the weight of all that came with it. For every new breakthrough begets a new breakdown in an endless cycle; in order to advance, we need to keep responding to the breakdowns not as failures but as opportunities in a never-ending cycle of innovation, renewal, and rediscovery within ourselves. I no longer give up at the failures but respond to every failure as a new opportunity in the way of self-improvement—the obstacle that becomes the way. My life sits atop a mountain of ashes—my own and those of others who sacrificed for me and cared for me, and for that, I am truly grateful and only hope that I can be that for my children and others and wish them the wherewithal I did not have, to recognize their failures as a gift!

Parting thought

I called this book about the virtues of failure *Beauty for Ashes* because I was so moved after listening to a sermon from Bishop T. D. Jakes about how the ashes represent God's redemptive power from the very beginning; legends in the Bible were known to put ashes on their heads as a sign of grief (Joshua 7:6). Job repented in ashes. God reduced the cities of Sodom and Gomorrah to ashes (2 Peter 2:6). Throughout Scripture, ashes signify our human condition. Ashes remind us that trials like failure and falling short produce humility, and sacrifices can bring about renewal. Beauty for ashes, or "a crown of beauty instead of ashes," is a scriptural promise detailed in Isaiah 61. Where it had been customary to don sackcloth and sit in ashes during times of grief and repentance, Isaiah announces that God has sent him to proclaim good news for the poor, freedom for prisoners, and comfort for the brokenhearted. He is describing the heart of the One who cleanses the ash from our lives and clothes us in the beautiful gift of salvation—the One who forgives our iniquities and remembers our sins no more (Hebrews 8:12). The ashes of grief, shame, and disgrace are exchanged with the reward of an everlasting covenant with God (Isaiah 61:8).

In Bishop Jakes's sermon titled "They Don't See the Ashes," Bishop Jakes tells of experiencing the ruins of Solomon's temple. It was David, Solomon's father, who sought to build this temple but had not completed it; the temple was built on Ornan's threshing floor from the previous generation, where David was trying to break a curse on his people by paying full price for the threshing floor even though he had the option of making an offer. The threshing floor is a place where wheat is separated from chaff. He goes on to say that in the previous generation, God judged David for his sins and let a plague come upon his people, and there was disaster, pestilence, and disease everywhere. David was trying to break the curse that was on the land and came to the threshing floor to make that sacrifice. According to Bishop Jakes, "People are always talking about your glory, but they don't know nothing about your story or what it costs."

All David was trying to do was stop the sword of the angel on his people, and the Bible said that he bought the threshing floor and burned it up to offer it up as a sacrifice to God. He points out that it was all built on ashes. Everything that Solomon built was built on the ashes that David burned; out of the ashes and the despair of his father's failures came his son's glory. Every son who had a failed father, out of his ashes came the glory of the next generation. We should stop despising our father's ashes because everything we will conceive during our lives will be built on the ashes our fathers left behind. The only reason Solomon owned the land was because David paid the full price for it. And David was wrestling with his own sins, and yet his sins and the place he wrestled for became the place where Solomon erected the first temple. So much of our success is built on our failures, our shortcomings, our ashes. In fact, if not for our failures, weaknesses, problems, mishaps, haters, and enemies, if not for all of it, we would not be who we are right here, right now, for the ashes. No, Solomon didn't get there by himself. It was not just his father's strengths, but it was also his weaknesses. Solomon wouldn't have been born if it were not for his father's weaknesses. Bishop Jake reminds us that Solomon's mother was his father's weakness, because Bathsheba, Solomon's mother, was somebody else's wife. If it had not been for his father's wrongs, Solomon would not have had right, so we should all stop crying about what went wrong because oftentimes, right on the backside of our mistake is our blessing, provided we have the sense of mind to learn from our failures. *Beauty for Ashes*, reminds us that although we may apologize for the mistakes, we should regret nothing because, as Bishop Jakes said, "my miracles are made out of my mistakes, and my successes are made out of my failures. And my victories are made out of my battles. And it was good for me that I was afflicted because I know my feet are flat on the ground, and I know everything I got it was built on ashes."

BIBLIOGRAPHY

Adelson, Eric. "Wie's Comeback Doomed Right from the Start." ESPN. May 31, 2007.

"A Revealing Experiment: Brown v. Board and 'The Doll Test.'" *Legal Defense Fund.* https://www.naacpldf.org/ldf-celebrates-60th-anniversary-brown-v-board-education/significance-doll-test/.

Bamberger, M. "Michelle Wie Gets DQ'd from Her First LPGA Event." golf.com. October 19, 2015.

Bradshaw, John. "Healing the Shame That Binds You," part one. PBS.

Bell, J. T. "Pyrrhic Victories." *The Military Engineer* 34, no. 197 (March 1942): 141.

Blass, R. "The Role of Tradition in Concealing and Grounding Truth: Two Opposing Freudian Legacies on Truth and Tradition." *American Imago* 63(3) (2006): 331–353. Accessed August 10, 2021. http://www.jstor.org/stable/26305348.

Boesveld, S. "Ashley Good: How One Woman Succeeded by Embracing Failure." Chatelaine. Accessed June 30, 2021. https://www.chatelaine.com/living/budgeting/how-one-woman-succeeded-by-embracing-failure/.

Brazillier, Z., "Former AAU Kingpin, Accused Child Molester Dead at Age 80." *New York Post*. 2012. https://nypost.com/2012/05/16/former-aau-kingpin-accused-child-molester-dead-at-age-80/.

Bryant, Sue. "How Do Different Cultures View Failure?" Accessed July 2, 2021. https://www.countrynavigator.com/blog/how-do-different-cultures-view-failure/.

Byrne, Rhonda. "How to Change the World using the Secret." https://www.thesecret.tv/blog/change-the-world/.

Campoamor, Diane. "No, Simone Biles Isn't a Quitter." *New York*. July 28, 2021. https://www.thecut.com/2021/07/olympics-2021-simone-biles-sexual-asault-survivors.html.

Cantopher, T., "The Power of Failure Developing Resilience in a Mad World." 2020.

"Career Summary." January 15, 2008 (archived from the original on November 20, 2008). https://twitter.com/michellewiefan.

Charles Manz. "The Power of Failure: 27 Ways to Turn Life's Setbacks into Success." 2002.

Connors, C. D. "How Steve Jobs' Biggest Failure Can Teach Us What It Means to Succeed." Ladders Fast on Your Feet. Accessed June, 24, 2021.

"Contending Wie Disqualified After Scorecard Error." ESPN. July 19, 2008.

Crouse, K. "Michelle Wie West Was Ready to Retire. Then She Got Mad." *New York Times.* Accessed June 29, 2021. https://www. nytimes.com/2021/06/03/sports/golf/lpga-michelle-wie-us-open.html.

Dileep, R. "What You Can Learn From Steve Jobs' Biggest Mistakes." *Forbes.* Accessed June 28, 2021. https://www.forbes.com/sites/dileeprao/2019/01/07/what-you-can-learn-from-steve-jobs-biggest-mistakes/?sh=76347de220b7.

Edwards, E. "Oprah Winfrey Admits Drug Use." *Washington Post.* January 13, 1995. https://www.washingtonpost.com/archive/politics/1995/01/13/oprah-winfrey-admits-drug-use/22391376-4674-463c-b4a0-efc6239ff9fb/.

Gardner, C. "I'm Chris Gardner. I'm an Entrepreneur, Single Parent and the Author of the 'Pursuit of Happyness.'" Chris Gardener Biography. Accessed June 29, 2021. https://www.chrisgardner-media.com/biography.

Goldenburg, S. "Why Women Are Poor at Science, by Harvard President." *Guardian.* January 18, 2005. https://www.theguardian.com/science/2005/jan/18/educationsgendergap.genderissues.

Good, A. "Fail Forward." Management Innovation Exchange. Accessed June 30, 2021. https://www.managementexchange.com/story/fail-forward.

Gracie, C. "Meet Ashley Good of Fail Forward: The World's First Failure Consultancy." Accessed June 30, 2021. https://editseven.ca/ashley-good-fail-forward-worlds-first-failure-consultancy/.

Gordon, D. "Chris Gardner: The Homeless Man Who Became a Multimillionaire Investor." BBC News. Accessed June 29, 2021. https://www.bbc.co.uk/news/business-38144980.

Hendricks, S. "Four Philosophers Who Realized They Were Completely Wrong about Things." Big Think. Accessed July 5, 2021. https://bigthink.com/scotty-hendricks/four-philosophers-who-realized-they-were-completely-wrong.

Hemel, D. J. "Summers' Comments on Women and Science Draw Ire, Remarks at Private Conference Stir Criticism, Media Frenzy." *The Harvard Crimson.* https://www.thecrimson.com/article/2005/1/14/summers-comments-on-women-and-science/.

"Hofstede Cultural Scales." Accessed July 10, 2021. https://www. hofstede-insights.com/country/jamaica/.

Holliday, R. "The Obstacle Is the Way: The Timeless Art of Turning Trials into Triumph." 2014.

Howard, J. "How Michelle Wie's Story Makes Us Rethink The Meaning Of Success." 2015. https://www.espn.com/espnw/ news-commentary/story/_/id/13195191/how-michelle-wie-story-makes-us-rethink-meaning-success.

Humphreys, T. "Effort, Failure, and Success." *Irish Times*. November 21, 2000. https://www.irishtimes.com/news/education/effort-failure-and-success-1.1116981.

"Intellectual Humility: The Ability to Know—and Admit—When You're Wrong." Accessed August 4, 2021. https://blog.arkadin. com/en/intellectual-humility-the-ability-to-know-and-admit-when-youre-wrong/.

Kedman, M. "Failure is Success."

Hyatt, Carole, and Linda Gottlieb. "When Smart People Fail." 1987.

London, A. "Why We Really Need to Talk About Simone Biles' Shocking Olympic Exit." Goalcast. Accessed August 3, 2021.

Loorbatch, D. "10 Things I Learned after Losing a Lot of Money." 2019. TEDxMünster. https://www.youtube.com/watch?v=_8l2egORXGA.

LPGA "Michelle Wie Profile and Statistics" (PDF). LPGA. December 23, 2006 (archived from the original PDF on February 16, 2007). Accessed July 6, 2021.

Lu, D., A. George, D. Cossins, and Layal Liverpool. "What You Experience May Not Exist: Inside the Strange Truth of Reality." *NewScientist*. Accessed July 27, 2021. http://affectivebrain.com/wp-content/uploads/2020/01/What-you-experience-may-not-exist.-Inside-the-strange-truth-of-reality-_-New-Scientist.pdf.

Luft, J., H. Ingham. "The Johari Window, a Graphic Model of Interpersonal Awareness" (proceedings of the western training laboratory in group development). Los Angeles: University of California, Los Angeles, 1955.

McNeil, L. "How a Psychologist's Work on Race Identity Helped Overturn School Segregation in 1950s America." 2017. https://www.smithsonianmag.com/science-nature/psychologist-work-racial-identity-helped-overturn-school-segregation-180966934/.

Marcin A. "What Is Atychiphobia and How Can You Manage Fear of Failure?" Healthline. Accessed June 21, 2021. https://www.healthline.com/health/atychiphobia.

Maharjan, B. "Failure and Self Awareness: Essential Mindfulness Skills to Thrive as Leaders." LinkedIn. Accessed June 23, 2021. https://www.linkedin.com/pulse/failure-self-awareness-bijay-maharjan-iamnepalese.

Mell, R. "Wie Sinks Incredible Birdie Putt at Last for Win in Singapore." GolfChannel.com. Accessed June 29, 2021. https://www.golfchannel.com/news/michelle-wie-ends-victory-drought-wins-dramatic-fashion-hsbc.

Nayfakh, L. "The Sadness of T-Pain." *New Yorker*. 2014. https://www.newyorker.com/culture/culture-desk/the-sadness-of-t-pain.

Newman, K. M., "Four Reasons to Cultivate Patience: Good Things Really Do Come to Those Who Wait." *Greater Good Magazine*. Accessed July 5, 2021. https://greatergood.berkeley.edu/article/item/four_reasons_to_cultivate_patience.

Niesen, J. "In a Divided US, It's No Surprise Some See Simone Biles as a Villain." *Guardian*. Accessed August 1, 2021. https://www.theguardian.com/sport/2021/jul/28/simone-biles-withdrawal-olympics-gymnastics-tokyo-media-reaction.

Nittle, N. "What Does It Mean to Be the Family Scapegoat." Verywell Mind. Accessed August 23, 2021. www.verywellmind.com.

Ojiako, U. and M. Chipulu. "National Culture and Perceptions of Success and Failure in Projects." Management Procurement and Law 167(4) (August 2014):167–179.

"Oops! Your Implicit Bias Is Showing." She Negotiates. April 16, 2014. https://www.shenegotiates.com/blog/2014/4/16/oops-your-implicit-bias-is-showing.

Pearl, Judea. "Heuristics: Intelligent Search Strategies for Computer Problem-Solving." New York: Addison-Wesley, 1983. vii. ISBN 978-0-201-05594-8.

Ramappa, A. "Why You Need Humility to Lead Through Change." Forbes. 2020. https://www.forbes.com/sites/forbescoachescouncil/2020/09/22/why-you-need-humility-to-lead-through-change/?sh=611dfd5a4d94.

Rana, Z. "J. K. Rowling: How to Deal With Failure." Observer. Accessed June 30, 2021. https://observer.com/2017/04/j-k-rowling-how-to-deal-with-failure/.

Reagan, S. "What Is The Law of Attraction and How Does It Work?" mindbodygreen. May 20, 2021. https://www.mindbodygreen.com/articles/the-law-of-attraction-simplified-what-it-is-and-how-to-use-it.

Robinson, R. "How Steve Jobs Learned to Embrace Failure and Saved Apple." The Balance Small Business. Accessed June 28, 2021. https://www.thebalancesmb.com/steve-jobs-and-how-embracing-failure-saved-apple-1200640.

Ruiz, D. M. "The Four Agreements: A Practical Guide to Personal Freedom" (Toltec wisdom book). 2018.

Sanchez, R. "Simone Biles Explains Competition Withdrawal at Olympics: 'My Mind and Body Are Simply Not in Sync.'" ABC News. Accessed August 1, 2021. https://abcnews.go.com/Sports/simone-biles-explains-withdrawal-olympics-mind-body-simply/story?id=79157744.

Scott, W. R. "Organizations and Organizing: Rational, Natural, and Open Systems Perspectives." Upper Saddle River, NJ: Prentice-Hall.

Shah, I. "The Sufis." New York: Anchor Books, 1971, pp. 2–15.

Sims, P. "Five of Steve Jobs's Biggest Mistakes." *Harvard Business Review*. 2013. https://hbr.org/2013/01/five-of-steve-jobss-biggest-mi.

Sisson, E. "J. K. Rowling: From Failure to Unimagined Success." *Writers College Times*. Accessed June 30, 2021. https://www.writerscollegeblog.com/j-k-rowling-from-failure-to-unimagined-success/.

Solomon, G. "'Jimmy The Greek' Fired by CBS for His Remarks." *Washington Post*. Accessed July 8, 2021. https://www.washingtonpost.com/archive/politics/1988/01/17/jimmy-the-greek-fired-by-cbs-for-his-remarks/27536e46-3031-40c2-bb2b-f912ec518f80/.

Spiegel, Alix. "Teachers' Expectations Can Influence How Students Perform." National Public Radio. 2012. https://www.npr.org/sections/health-shots/2012/09/18/161159263/teachers-expectations-can-influence-how-students-perform.

Stevens, E. "Why Taking a Hit Is the Best Way to Avoid a Hit." Breaking Muscle. Accessed June 22, 2021. https://breakingmuscle.com/fitness/why-taking-a-hit-is-the-best-way-to-avoid-a-hit.

Stocke, K. "Knowing When It's Time to Give Up." The Tiny Buddha: Simple Wisdom for Complex Times. Accessed June 27, 2021. https://tinybuddha.com/blog/how-to-know-when-its-time-to-give-up/.

Stibel, J. "Michael Jordan: A Profile in Failure." CSQ. Accessed June 24, 2021. https://csq.com/2017/08/michael-jordan-profile-failure/#.YNpBCS9Q3BV.

Strozzi-Heckler, R. "In Search of the Warrior Spirit: Teaching Awareness Disciplines to the Military." 4th ed. Blue Snake Books.

The Psychology of Risk and Reward (website blog). Accessed June 24, 2021. https://fs.blog/2015/10/the-psychology-of-risk-and-reward/.

Tinsley, J. "T-Pain Popularized Auto-Tune, but It Came at a Cost." https://theundefeated.com/features/t-pain-popularized-auto-tune-but-it-came-at-a-cost/.

Tulshyan, Ruchika, and Jodi-Ann Burey. "Stop Telling Women They Have Imposter Syndrome." *Harvard Business Review*. Accessed July 10, 2021. https://hbr.org/2021/02/stop-telling-women-they-have-imposter-syndrome.

"Twelve-Year-Old Misses Cut, but Not the Fun." ESPN. Associated Press, March 1, 2002.

Wanderlust Worker. "48 Famous Failures Who Will Inspire You to Achieve." Accessed June 29, 2021. https://www.wanderlustworker.com/48-famous-failures-who-will-inspire-you-to-achieve/.

Weiss, D. C. "Partners in study gave legal memo a lower rating when told author wasn't white." *ABA Journal* (2014). Accessed

August 1, 2021. https://www.abajournal.com/news/article/hypothetical_legal_memo_demonstrates_unconscious_biases.

"Why Winning Doesn't Always Equal Success | Valorie Kondos Field" (video). Accessed June 25, 2021. https://www.youtube.com/watch?v=JJyeKiT8g4g.

Willingham, D. T. "Ask the Cognitive Scientist: Practice Makes Perfect—but Only If You Practice beyond the Point of Perfection." Accessed June 26, 2021. https://www.aft.org/periodical/american-educator/spring-2004/ask-cognitive-scientist-practice-makes-perfect.

"Windrush: Post-War Immigration 1948." British Library. https://www.bl.uk/learning/timeline/item107829.html; NPR. Retrieved 2019-03-31.

Winograd, T., and F. Flores. "Understanding Computers and Cognition: A New Foundation for Design." Addison-Wessley Publishing Company Inc., 1990.

Wrosch, C., M. Scheier, C. Carver, and R. Schulz. "The Importance of Goal Disengagement in Adaptive Self-Regulation: When Giving Up is Beneficial Self and Identity." Psychology Press. 2003. 1529-8868/2003.

W. Richard Scott and G.F. Davis (2007), "Organizations and Organizing: Rational, Natural and Open Systems Perspectives" Routlage, Taylor and Francis Group

"You Need to Be Punched in the Face." Freestyle Taekwondo Federation. Accessed June 22, 2021. https://www.freestyle-taekwondofederation.com/single-post/2017/02/10/you-need-to-be-punched-in-the-face.

ABOUT THE AUTHOR

 Dr. Pierre N. McDonnaugh, JD, LLM, holds a DPS from the Pace University Lubin School of Business, in Economics and International Management, an LLM from the American University Washington College of Law, in Law and Government and is a graduate of Howard University School of Law and a Connecticut licensed Attorney practicing in the area of banking, compliance, and financial derivatives regulation. He is also a self-professed *Professional Failure—as knowing "how to fail" is the true path to success in any endeavor.*

Lightning Source UK Ltd.
Milton Keynes UK
UKHW011858041222
413331UK00001B/13